The Girl's Guide to Being a Boss

Valuable lessons and smart suggestions for making the most of managing

Caitlin Friedman and Kimberly Yorio

A & C Black • London

First published in the United States by Morgan Road Books, an imprint of The Doubleday Broadway Publishing Group, a division of Random House, Inc.

First published in Great Britain by A & C Black Publishers Ltd, 38 Soho Square, London W1D 3HB

British Library Cataloguing in Publication Data
A CIP record for this book is available from the British Library.

ISBN-10: 0-7136-7709-0
ISBN-13: 978-0-7136-7709-6

A & C Black uses paper produced with elemental chlorine-free pulp, harvested from managed sustainable forests.

Design by Fiona Pike, Pike Design, Winchester
Typeset by Palimpsest Book Production Ltd, Grangemouth, Stirlingshire
Printed in the United Kingdom by Bookmarque

Contents

Introduction

While writing our first book, *The Girl's Guide to Starting Your Own Business*, we had to edit the chapter entitled 'Being a Boss Sucks' down from an unreasonable 200 pages. Why so long? Because we had both struggled with the leadership role since hiring our first assistant and had a lot to say about its challenges, as did most of the women we interviewed. The upshot; managing is hard. Over the past year our little public relations agency has tripled in size, raising a stack of questions we hadn't faced before. Who do you promote? Who do you fire? How do you effectively train an employee? How long do you invest in employees before you can expect them to pay off? How do you demonstrate gratitude for a job well done without going broke? But the biggest question that we have struggled with – and continue to do so on an almost daily basis – is how to own and enjoy the role of boss lady.

After a lot of thought – and even more research – we've come to learn that too many women in the work force (including us!) haven't had the chance to learn from positive female role models. Without positive experiences to draw from, we've ended up repeating bad behaviour. We are hoping that this book will provide the insight and positive reinforcements so many of us have searched for in our own professional lives.

With some introspection, research, and interviews with lots of ladies who lead, we have come to the conclusion that women actually have it in them to be better managers than their male counterparts. If we could just get over our fears, the traits we are born with as women – nurturing, patience, strength, wisdom, and resourcefulness – are the very characteristics that will make us stars in the boardroom and the mentor many employees are hoping for.

We are empowering you, by adopting the role of queen bee in a positive way, to become that one-in-a-million manager. You can be powerful with out being possessive. You can be opinionated without being brassy. You can have a strong voice without micromanaging. You can be a mentor who leads, inspires, and motivates.

There is no fast track to owning this role, or even getting better at it, but we think after reading *The Girl's Guide to Being a Boss* you will be well on your way.

You're a Big Girl Now: From Just Another Employee to Chick in Charge

O K. So you're the boss now. The supervisor. The manager. The captain. The taskmaster. Those days of taking orders, running errands, and clock-watching are over forever. At last, you get to call the shots.

As exciting as all this might seem, once the rush of the promotion is over, you might be scratching your head wondering exactly what your new responsibility entails. Many of us haven't had positive role models and feel a little lost once we arrive at the grown-up table. Fear not. You know you can do the job; all you need is a little helpful advice to send you on your way.

Whether you manage two people as a shift manager or lord it over an entire corporate empire, we'll help you to take the leap from mediocre to marvellous. And for those of you who are already running the show, we can help you to lose that nickname, 'Bitch on Wheels', and become the leader your employees deserve.

We'll show you what it means to be queen: how to wield your ever-evolving bag of management tricks; how to discover what is expected of you; how to decide what you can reasonably expect of your team; and how to jump in and love every minute of your Head Honchoness. You've earned this, baby. Enjoy!

Good Days and Bad Days: The Good, Bad, and Ugly Aspects of Being a Manager

Leading can be a daunting task. In some ways it can be positively thrilling. In others, it can be a pain in the backside. Just as the freedom, responsibility, and respect start to lift you to cloud nine, the paranoia, fear, and anxiety can bring you crashing back down to earth. Like all things, being the recognized leader can have its highs and lows. Here's a look at the lawns on both sides of the fence.

The good

Money, money, money, money, MONEY!

We might be dreaming, but, if you've been promoted, we'd like to assume a nice pay rise came along with it. Hopefully you'll have to struggle less to make ends meet or face your credit card bills at the end of the month. Even if the new job doesn't mean a giant windfall, being the boss should put you in a better financial position than you were before. And, if you're not, make sure you find out the going rate and lobby for what you deserve.

Princess of power

Power is good. Making decisions that lead to positive outcomes is good. Making the calls, changing the rules, and forging decisions that may alter the course of the entire company can be great. Having the ultimate responsibility is positively thrilling.

The bitch boss who throws her weight around, barks orders, and is generally focused on herself while making her employees miserable doesn't have to be you. Once you settle into your new role, you'll find that being the leader means you can be the manager who boosts employees and gets real enjoyment from watching her colleagues grow and prosper. Building a team, working together, and teaching others will be hugely gratifying. At the end of the day, it can make you feel like a million dollars.

The more you know

While mentoring your dewy protégés, you yourself will be acquiring new information and facing fresh and exciting challenges everyday. Acquired knowledge changes us and makes us better mothers, friends, and businesswomen. Growing professionally can be empowering and give you a broader perspective on both the world and your place within it. The more you know the better off you are, both intellectually and when it comes to updating your CV. Don't forget the journey to becoming a great leader is a life-long one.

Your mum will be proud

Ultimately, if you succeed, the prestige and glow of success will make all the mistakes and missteps worthwhile. There is no greater feeling in the world than a job well done.

The bad

Training, anyone?

The sad reality is there's never enough training offered to employees. Even in a company with well-established training programmes, there will be plenty of times when you just don't know what to do. You would think that when a new person is hired she would be handed all the necessary tools to do her job effectively. Maybe the person before you fled the job or was fired, and the people who remain don't really know what she did.

Perhaps everyone is too busy to sit down and go through your job in detail. Whatever the reason, your training will probably consist of 'Here's your office. Good luck.' It's up to you to work out how to achieve your goals using the best resource you have – your staff.

It's lonely at the top

For all of the positive things your new role as a manager can bring, probably the scariest downside of the whole thing is the isolation you will feel as the woman at the top of the corporate ladder. You have the responsibility to make your team a success, and, if it fails, you take the blame. Gone are the days when you can be everyone's friend. No more shuffling off to the canteen to spend an hour having a good natter about the latest episode of *Desperate Housewives*. When asked the biggest mistake that new managers make, 90% of the women we interviewed replied that they try to be liked. You are not there to be anyone's friend. You are in the leadership role to provide the tools and environment that your team needs to accomplish their goals. If the team is not accomplishing the goals, with all the appropriate support, then you, new manager, will have to reprimand and maybe dismiss team members who aren't measuring up. The power that you gain when promoted will separate you from your team.

Keep the personal personal, and never let them see you sweat

This is a tough one. No matter how bad it gets, no matter what kind of a day you're having, you absolutely, positively cannot freak out. It doesn't matter if your car died in the middle of the motorway on your way to work, or that you just found out your husband has been having an affair. Your personal problems should not come into the workplace. At Ann's first job as an assistant, her boss was trying to adopt a baby. She had a special mobile phone just for potential birth mothers to call. When her boss was in a meeting, Ann was required to man the baby phone. If a potential birth mother called, Ann would have to find her boss. If her boss couldn't be disturbed, she would have to interview the potential birth mother and try to schedule a time for a return call. Ann was flattered at the amount of trust put in her by her boss, but scared to death that, if she messed up the baby phone, not only was she jeopardizing her job, she could potentially cause her boss to the lose the baby she was so desperately trying to get. While adopting a baby was obviously the priority for her boss, it was unfair to make it the focus of Ann's day.

The buck stops with you

The team's problems are now your problems – individually and collectively. As a matter of fact, everyone's problems become your problems. If a member of your group has a sick child and can't be there for the ten o'clock meeting with the biggest client, then you have to find a way to cover for her without the client ever knowing. If your top account executive loses the biggest account, and your department won't make its numbers, then *you* will have to find a replacement account or shrink the team to cover the shortfall. And, at the very least, you will have to take the heat from your management. If someone on your team opens an e-mail from her boyfriend that infects your entire office with a virus, erasing all your records from the last five years, then you and the IT department have a very big problem. No more hiding until the storm blows over. It will be your responsibility to mobilize the team, board up the windows, and evacuate.

Discipline, warnings, and wielding the axe

Delivering bad news is never easy; deciding to severely damage someone's livelihood by sacking them because they can't cut the mustard is no picnic. We've devoted almost an entire chapter (7) to the 'f' word – firing.

The ugly

Nowhere to go but down

With each step you climb up the corporate ladder, the further down you will go if you fall off. You will exist in constant fear of not living up to expectations (although the rest of the group shouldn't know it), of not getting the job done effectively, or of not accomplishing the team's goals. The higher you go, the more you're under scrutiny from those beneath you who think they can do your job better and those above you who think they are paying you too much. If you don't create positive relationships from the word go, those go-getters will take every opportunity to prove that they are more suited to your job. We're not suggesting you become paranoid, but we do suggest that you remain aware of the changing dynamics of your senior position. In Chapter 2, we will explore why management experts recommend forging relationships with those above, below and equal to you in the organization.

The Rap Sheet: Celluloid Bitch Bosses

1. *Kill Bill* (2003). Lucy Liu as O-Ren Ishii, the evil crime boss of Tokyo's underworld. When one of her peers questions her leadership, she cuts his head off without missing a beat.
Lesson: You need to have an open door policy for all your employees so they can speak their mind. Firing or reprimanding someone just for disagreeing with you is unacceptable, though you shouldn't be a push-over either.

2. *Disclosure* (1994). Demi Moore as Meredith Johnson. She comes on to her employee then acts as if he sexually harassed her. Evil ensues through lies and cover-ups.

Lesson: *Never, ever* flirt with an employee, and never use sex to leverage your power. Granted, Demi's problems in this movie go deeper than that, but your own sexuality should never come into play in the workplace.

3. *Working Girl* (1988). Sigourney Weaver as Katharine Parker. She steals her employee's idea, but gets it in the end when her employee steals her life.
Lesson: Never take credit for a colleague's hard work. You'll look like a bitch and lose the trust of your employees, not to mention that you might find yourself as the target of a good case of revenge.

4. *Truth or Dare* (1991). Madonna as herself. In this documentary of the material girl, she is revealed as the worst kind of boss. She exerts a sort of maternal control over her dancers, going from being their best friend to being a total bitch.
Lesson: Bipolar Betty has no place in the office. You have to remain consistent, loyal and unbiased with all your employees no matter how how badly they screw up.

5. *Raising Helen* (2004). Helen Mirren as Dominique. As the boss of a modelling agency, when her employee inherits her sister's kids, she proves the work place is less than family friendly by stealing her clients and belittling her in front of the staff for being late to a meeting.
Lesson: Yes, you have to think of the company's wellbeing first, but in the end it is the staff that is the company. As long as the work is getting done, you can create a positive and flexible work environment for your team.

6. *101 Dalmatians* **(1996).** Glenn Close as Disney über-villainess Cruella de Vil. Not only is she a puppy killer, in this version of the classic cartoon she terrorizes her employees at her fashion design firm by screaming, throwing things, and generally humiliating all of those who work for her.

Lesson: Never lead with fear. It is possible to have a firm hand and still enjoy the respect of your colleagues. Using terror tactics is never the way to make your office function efficiently. Firm but fair is the way to go.

7. *Catwoman* **(2004).** Sharon Stone as Laurel Hedare. When her employee discovers that the 'miracle' anti-aging face cream her cosmetics company makes has terrible side-effects, Laurel resorts to murder to prevent her from revealing the truth.

Lesson: Firstly, never lie to your employees. Secondly, if you do, be ready to face the repercussions when the truth is revealed.

The Job: Key Functions and Roles

Though the responsibilities of any management job can vary wildly depending what on business you're in, there are a few elemental duties you'll be asked to perform that translate across the board. We'll touch on these here first, but go into each in greater detail in later chapters.

You will hire, fire, evaluate, and promote

Putting together your team and keeping it in line will be your most important role as a manager. You will need to decide if additional employees are needed and can be afforded. You must be constantly accessible to the ones you have and evaluate them.

If the creative department is swamped, staying late every night, and bickering because they are burned out, it is up to you to decide how to help ease the workload.

In our research, the single biggest criticism we heard about women managers is that they are too emotional. They should just be more professional. After all, business is just business. But is it? Business is actually done through the coming together of a number of individuals with very different styles and personalities. As a manager, you will have to find a way to make them as productive as they can possibly be.

Hiring, firing, evaluating, and promoting are the most emotional decisions you can make. Take recruitment, for example. A responsible HR manager will solicit a number of CVs, prune them down to the top candidates, interview the candidates a few times, check references, and then make a decision. When faced with a few candidates with similar strengths, how do you choose? You try to assess who will be the best personality fit for the group and hope for the best.

When it doesn't work out, then you have to fire. And don't tell us that firing employees isn't an emotional exercise. You are taking away a person's livelihood and perhaps that of their family too. Emotions come into play. The trick for a woman is to be able to manage her emotions as well as she manages her staff. Consistency is the best you can hope for and is probably good enough to keep the emotional criticism out of the office.

You will have a plan and delegate work to your employees

For those times when your staff isn't in flux, creating a business plan and delegating its various aspects will be your main managerial task. This includes earmarking what needs to be accomplished on a daily, weekly, monthly, yearly, and long-term basis; making a schedule; and determining who on your team is best to handle each assignment. You will be asking questions such as 'Is this a one-person job?' Would putting your workers into teams be more productive?

Delegating doesn't just mean telling your team what to do. You have to make sure they understand the project and how best to achieve its goals. Communication is the only way to make sure everyone stays on schedule. Checking in on a regular basis through progress reports and being involved will ensure the job gets done right.

Every manager has to delegate but, according to www.advancingwomen.com, many women are reluctant to do so. They cite a number of reasons including:

- Most of us succeed because we are good at mastering certain types of details.
- It's human nature to like to do what we're good at doing.
- Successful women are often perfectionists.
- If we do it ourselves, we know it will be perfect, or, at least, as perfect as we can make it.

You will provide guidance, direction, motivation, and inspiration to your employees

When a long-time employee comes to you with questions on how a new system works, you will be the woman who listens intently to the problem and ultimately provides the answers. Say one of your salespeople feels the company's current marketing techniques aren't quite bringing the customers in. She arrives at your office door with a load of new ideas. At this point, your direction is imperative, and together you can sort the problem out and make the right decision.

Or let's imagine profits are down, the competition is taking you to the cleaners, and morale in the office is at an all-time low. This is your opportunity to lead, to motivate, to inspire, and to make your staff believe in the product/company/mission with a passion they've never felt before. Call in a research firm to help to identify why it is that your competitor has the edge, and then lead a brainstorming session to develop ways to respond. Organize a group retreat where everyone can come together and air their issues and problems; then work together to find a solution. Providing guidance and inspiration to your staff will be the most challenging part of your job, but ultimately the most fulfilling.

You will supervise and maintain the financial health of the company and/or department

Whether you are given a budget to follow or have to create guidelines from scratch, it will be your responsibility to stay within the parameters of the planned spending. If your department has a quarterly budget of £200,000, your job is to allocate resources so that you come in under or on that planned spending limit. Be prepared to explain why if you don't.

Managing budgets can include finding ways to cut back on staff if your payroll is ballooning, or shifting monies from one project to another if one needs additional funding. It will also mean finding new ways to boost your profit margin so that your bottom line is expanded. If you have never had to handle money before, you will be working it like a casino dealer before you know it.

You will be expected to answer for your staff, department, or branch

No matter what level of leader you are, you will still have to answer to someone. If you're an entrepreneur, ultimately your customers will have the last word if the quality of your product starts to falter. In most managerial jobs there is someone above you calling the shots, whether you are a district manager, branch supervisor, or the head of your department. You will be expected to answer up the chain of command. You have to be confident when dealing with senior management and defend your department or take responsibility for missteps. Just as you need to communicate with your employees, you must keep an open line between you and your boss.

You will act as a buffer between your employees and any management above you

Your top store manager screwed up the product returns, leaving your area with a deficit of £50,000. When the boss finds out and comes down on you like a ton of bricks, you have to take the brunt of the hit, yet pass it down in a way that is productive and supportive to your employees. No matter how badly the chairman of the board might behave towards you, you can't pass that negative attitude down. You are responsible for the actions of your staff. Hopefully in delegation and direction, you've made the right decisions; so whatever goes wrong, you are largely to blame. Any antagonistic energy you get from above has to be recycled into positive change.

Good Witch or Big Bitch?

Minimum tasks, maximum humiliation

When Jenny was looking for a career change she was thrilled to read that a local public relations company was in need of a publicity assistant. Even better, the owner of the agency was reputed to be one of the best in the business, a real dynamo and a great person to learn from. The interview was a breeze, and Jenny was promised lots of opportunities, including working with the media. The trade-off, her future boss would tell her, was that 'you will have to run the office, which shouldn't take more than a few hours a week'. By the end of her first week, it was clear that what she would actually be doing was running the office while squeezing in a few media calls during her lunch breaks.

Jenny could handle the bait and switch. What she couldn't handle was the treatment she received from the owner of the business. On top of the choice assignments – cleaning the storeroom, ordering pens and other office supplies, returning her boss's rented videos to a local shop, packing and shipping hundreds of items every week – three or four times a day the owner of the business would hop on the office-wide intercom to demand that Jenny run up to her office to clean out her outbox. Every time Jenny heard the three beeps indicating a page, her stomach would drop because she knew that it meant passing her colleagues – busy talking on their phones – on her way to pick up a pile of personal notes and to-do lists waiting for her in the outbox.

Jenny's downfall? She was too good at her job. A model of efficiency, she got the office running like clockwork. She updated the files and negotiated phone rates, and everyone was happy. Except Jenny. As the weeks went by, her colleagues picking up on the demeaning manner in which she was treated by the owner, began taking advantage of her too. Her contribution to Monday morning meetings was soon taking supply orders from the rest of the staff. The media call assignments became increasingly infrequent as her day became filled with padded envelopes and paper clips. When she confronted the owner of the business, she replied, 'give it time, now here's my outbox.'

Jenny lasted eight months at the job, wanting to have something to add to her CV, but hating every day of it. More than that, she hated her boss.

Big Bitch. The most important job of a manager is to inspire and keep good employees. Jenny was a superstar. She handled her assignments with efficiency and good cheer. The staff liked and respected her until they watched her manager belittle her accomplishments and devalue her contribution by interrupting her to sort her mail. Jenny could have been a key member of the team for years to come; instead, she quit as soon as she could find another boss.

A Definition of Management

From *The American Heritage Dictionary* (Third Edition), Houghton Mifflin:

management 1. The act, manner, or practice of managing; handling, supervision, or control. 2. The person or persons who control or direct a business or other enterprise.

manager 1. One who handles, controls or directs.

Even the dictionary tells you, managing is about control. But controlling people is never as easy as it should be. Women be wary.

Movin' On Up: New Expectations

Now that you're in a management role, you will no longer have someone looking over your shoulder and telling you what to do every minute of the day; no one is responsible for you except you. Acknowledging your job responsibilities will be the key to your ultimate success.

Here are 15 things you should always do now that you are responsible for yourself and your team.

1. **Create a to-do list**
   Since no one will be delegating to you, it is up to you to keep an eye on what needs to be done. Creating a to-do list is one of the best ways to prioritize and keep track. With a

list to refer to, small things will never fall through the cracks and you'll always have the next step at your fingertips.

2. Set goals

What do you want to accomplish in your new position? More than anyone, you know what you are capable of, and it is up to you to set goals not just for yourself but for the company as a whole. Set goals and stick with them. Daily, monthly, even long-term planning can mean the difference between what does and does not get done.

3. Stick to deadlines

A deadline is a deadline. A promise to a client to have a commercial developed, cast, and filmed by a certain date should be set in stone. A date ultimatum from the head office for the grand opening of the new store should be treated as gospel. A pledge to your staff to complete performance appraisals before the end of the month should be met even if it means working late over a Bank Holiday to get it done. If *you* can't keep to a deadline, how can you expect your employees to do the same?

4. Keep your word

A new employee is promised a pay rise in six months during contract negotiations. A customer is offered a full refund if the face cream they ordered doesn't make them look ten years younger. A peer asks if you'll take her report home over the weekend and get it back to her before she has to show it to your boss on Monday. When you say you are going to do something, make sure you do it. Nothing is worth more in business than trust.

5. Get it in writing

Now that you are responsible for others, make sure that

they are all clear about their objectives. The easiest way to make sure everyone knows what is happening is to put it all down on paper.

6. **Be proactive about everything you do**
Don't wait for directions and a map; get to work. If your team is assigned a project that is new, sit down together and work out how to get it done. If a new advertising plan for your company seems to be backfiring, find out how to fix it. Don't sit idly by.

7. **Treat your aspect of the business like an entrepreneur**
Understanding what everyone in your department does will ensure that you always know what is going on. Let's say shoplifting in your stores is on the rise; work with the security team to come up with ways to prevent it. Don't think about your business unit or responsibilities individually, but think about how you can contribute to the bigger picture.

8. **Contribute to the team**
Not only must you pull your own weight, but you must prove to the staff that you're not afraid to get your hands dirty. Acting as part of the troupe will not only help you to run your business more effectively; it will also win you the respect of those above you, below you, and across from you.

9. **Think big picture**
Up until this point in your career, you've been asked to take on one task and work closely on the details. As you move up the corporate ladder, you'll become more focused on the big picture, while the team supporting you should be obsessing over the details.

10. Be your own cheerleader

Being the boss can be a thankless job. No one is going to hold your hand and tell you what a great job you're doing any more. You have to depend on yourself for a pat on the back. When you've worked hard and accomplished a goal, take yourself out to lunch, get a massage, or arrange for a day out of the office.

11. Sell your accomplishments to those above you

No one is going to be there to witness when you do something amazing. Don't be afraid to blow your own trumpet to your higher ups. If you are uncomfortable selling yourself, use the opportunity to pump up the team. Not only will this make your team look hot, it will endear you to your boss as a great leader. If you don't work it for yourself, who will?

12. Stick up for yourself

In the past, you possibly had someone looking out for you when things got rough or someone tried to pass an undeserved buck in your direction. More than likely, you won't have that person now. If you feel you are being unfairly treated, don't feel too intimidated to make a stand. Again, if you don't, who will?

13. Don't take things personally

Geraldine Ferraro was once in the frame for running for U.S. president. She might still have a vibrant political career if she hadn't taken some partisan bashing to heart and wept in front of the American public. You have to have thick skin in the business world and realize that just because someone gets angry, or you get passed over for a rise, or your management hands a project to another district manager, it doesn't mean you're rubbish. Handle disappointments with class. Remember, this advice swings both ways; there will be days when you have to discipline a friend or take an able worker off an account because they haven't pulled their weight. Business is business.

14. **Don't forget to network**
Building alliances is what helps people win on reality game shows, and it is what you will need to do in order to make it in the rough and tumble world of business. Meet as many people in and out of your field as you can. Spend your time building positive perceptions and do anything you can to help others out. The more people who respect you as a professional, the better off you'll be when you need to call in a favour. Not only will these people be able to help you out at one point or another, but they'll also be a valuable support group, and in some cases they will even become lifelong friends.

15. **Find a mentor**
Seek out someone in your company or in your field who has more experience than you – someone you can learn from, someone who might be willing to take you under her wing and impart all her worldly wisdom. Making this kind of connection early on can help you through the best and worst of times. Nothing beats having someone you can go to for managerial advice and support.

The Word: Linda Brierty, Therapist

Why do you think that women are so afraid of being perceived as a bitch in the workplace?
Without perpetuating gender stereotypes, let me address this. Some women may fear their own power and

leadership, and this power is not always encouraged, or even allowed in certain settings. Strong women may be viewed as intimidating. There may be actual negative consequences for speaking up.

Many women have been conditioned to want acceptance and approval from others, at times to their own self-detriment. This relates to the historical role of caring for others and neglecting themselves. Self-advocacy and self-care – all those 'self' words in fact – may have been perceived as 'selfish'.

It is commonly known that when a woman behaves like her male counterparts in the workplace, she is often negatively labelled. If she is assertive or stands her ground, she is called tough. If she is matter-of-fact and not emotional, she is cold. The expectations are skewed by gender, despite the progress that has been made. This can discourage assertive behaviour and effectively keep women down, even in the present day. Because we may respond to the world emotionally as well as intellectually, it may be hard to separate our feelings from the work itself. We may fear rejection or have dependency issues, including the need to be liked and part of the group. This may supercede acknowledging our own power.

Do you have any advice for first time managers on how they can begin to overcome their fears about telling others what to do?
First time managers can remind themselves that this is not school. This is not a popularity contest, although a firm grasp of people skills is extremely important. If you alienate your staff, your productivity will suffer. If everyone is motivated, it will soar. Remember, employees are people will feelings. Using constructive feedback

instead of personal criticism is important. Leaving everyone's self-esteem intact is crucial.

When you are delegating or instructing someone, it's all about the facts. You are simply trying to get a job done. It is not personal, and it is wise to move the emotions out of the way and keep discussion matter-of-fact and productive. If there is a problem, identify it as an issue to be resolved, not as a vehicle for character assassination. You can then develop solutions to leave the conversation on a high note. It is also important to identify employees' strengths. You should anticipate a degree of anger and resentment from employees, simply by virtue of the role of authority you find yourself in. It goes with the territory. Be flattered. Remember you will also be a lightning conductor for employees' transferential reactions, meaning feelings from previous relationships with authority figures will be projected onto you. Don't take it personally, don't respond personally.

Owning your power means leading others in a respectful way. You will not always be liked; however, you will need to be respected to maintain your authority in the position. You will need to establish and maintain professional boundaries with people. Be prepared: it can be lonely. You will not be able to be part of the peer group. You will be talked about.

Do you have any confidence boosters for women – things they can think about or do to feel good about themselves?
You have to summon up confidence in yourself because of all your wonderful qualities. You have to maintain a supportive inner dialogue. Turn off the inner critic and don't be so hard on yourself. If you don't do that, the

world can knock you over more easily. If you act and speak on your own behalf, you are taking care of yourself. Remember, we are trained to take care of others; so this is a conscious reversal. We are no longer the exception to our own care and attention. There is nothing wrong with liking yourself, encouraging yourself – this is not a deadly sin of pride. Our light shines brighter this way, and we can refuse to turn down our flame for anyone. When you get beyond your own ego you can actually do more in and for the world.

No Free Time?: Balancing Home, Family, and Friends

It's easy to get caught up in the thrill of doing a good job, working your fingers to the bone, putting in long hours, and driving into the office at the weekend. We once had a boss who kept handwritten crayon signs by her desk that read, 'Remember, Mum, family comes first'. We never wanted to be those kinds of friends or mothers, and we've made a conscious effort to find the right balance between our private and working lives. Here are a few thoughts on how to have a social and home life and still get the job done.

Organize your time at home

The better you organize your time at home, the more time you will have to spend with your family and friends. Make lists and keep schedules so that home duties can run just as efficiently as the ones you have at work. Some great calendar programs are available on-line that allow you to input the entire family's schedules, including the nanny, and it will automatically send reminders for car pools and doctor's appointments. This is especially helpful with divorced parents as it offers a neutral place for all parties to keep track of the schedule. We recommend www.ourfamilywizard.com.

Don't forget your friends

Friendships can often be just as important as family life. It's a total release to get together with your girlfriends and pretend you're sixteen again. If you find it difficult to catch up with them, plan a monthly girls' night and make a pact to always be there, no matter what. We have a monthly book group that has been meeting for years, and, as we have all gone up the ladder at our jobs, the conversations have moved from complaining about our bosses to the challenges of being a boss. Kim goes to a girls' weekend twice a year with her old school friends and will often extend a business trip with a Saturday night stay if she is in a city where she has a friend. Your employer won't mind, because the reduced cost of the airfare generally more than covers the cost of an extra night in a hotel

Stay upbeat

No matter how hairy things get at work or how crazy life can be at home, try and keep a positive outlook. Nothing wastes time and zaps energy more than a bad attitude. Believe us, it's not always easy. When we're really down and frustrated with work, we focus our energy on turning a negative into a positive. We like results. For example, if we're feeling the pressure of no cash flow in the business, we devote 20 minutes each to collections, calling and e-mailing clients to remind them to pay our overdue bills. This little exercise cheers us up in a number of ways: firstly, we get the benefit about feeling good about solving a problem; secondly, we immediately see the light at the end of the tunnel, because we know when the money is coming in; and, thirdly, it reinvigorates us to go out and get new business, because we love getting paid.

If we're feeling pressured that we're not generating enough

exposure for a client, we'll stop everything, and each of us will spend 20 minutes pitching new media outlets. Invariably we secure a placement, and, again, we are cheered up at having made a positive change to our situation.

Make time for you

Most important of all, you have to carve out time for yourself; otherwise, you will never be able to juggle everything and still maintain your sanity. Wake up a half hour earlier than the rest of your family to enjoy that first cup of coffee in peace. Steal away to a yoga class for a midday detox.

2

The Big Picture:
What It Takes to Become
a Great Leader

*I*t's not easy for women to become great leaders. Forces actually conspire against them. Since the early 1980s, studies (Porter, Geis, & Jennings, 1983) have shown that what works for men doesn't work for women in a leadership context. Those studies also show that women are not socialized to become leaders and that great leading female role models are few and far between. Of course, there's Eleanor Roosevelt, Hillary Clinton, Madeleine Albright, Oprah Winfrey, and Maya Angelou, but, beyond that, can you name anyone? On the Internet the only site devoted to women leaders through history is a personal one called www.guide2womenleaders.com and it's written and maintained by a Danish *man*!

Whether you've just been promoted or are planning for the future, now is the time to make sure you have the right stuff to be a great boss, not just a good one. But where do you begin?

This is not an easy or quick process. For most, it will take a lifetime of work to become an admired and valuable leader. You must adopt effective strategies and habits now that will set you on the right path. What's most important, though, is to monitor your progress and continue to learn and grow.

Why Being the Boss Isn't Always a Bummer: What's In It for You?

Think about how great you feel when you accomplish something, when you get that rush for a job well done. Crossing things off the to-do list has to be one of the most satisfying things in anyone's day. Now, multiply that feeling by five, ten, or maybe even 100 – that's the big pay-off for bosses and leaders. Your job as leader or manager is to facilitate others' accomplishments. Leaders give the direction, support, inspiration, or space for the subordinate to accomplish her goals.

We are led to believe that leading is the most natural skill in the world, but we're here to tell you that, not only is leading not natural for most, it's damn difficult for everyone. Neither one of us is a shrinking violet, yet we find it challenging to assert our authority without feeling like the world's biggest bitches.

Leadership implies a relationship. Someone leads and someone follows. And, as women know better than anyone, relationships are complicated. The other side rarely reacts as you think they will, and you need to constantly learn from your mistakes. Here's a good example.

Good Witch or Big Bitch?

Firm but fair

We hired a new assistant in our office. We went through a rigorous interviewing process and found an incredibly energetic, smart, and enthusiastic young woman. We explained her initial responsibilities and set her off to work. We agreed that we would spend time with her – a little bit individually each day – and copy her in on much of our e-mail correspondence, but we found ourselves on some crazy deadlines; so we told her she would need to learn as much as possible by listening and asking questions. We didn't have much time for teaching (not good management, by the way). After all, we were incredibly busy with the 'important' work, pitching new business, running the office, and servicing the existing clients. Our assistant was there to make our lives easier, and not vice versa. We were unknowingly furthering a model we had suffered under in the early part of our careers. We were scared to death at our first jobs because our bosses had thrown us into the deep end of the pool. The sink or swim style of management stinks. Even the most resourceful employee will become frustrated and make mistakes.

Ten days into the job, a series of unfortunate events occurred. Kim was in Paris for a long weekend, and Caitlin was holding the fort. The Internet inexplicably went down, which obviously can be disastrous to any small business. When Kim returned from holiday, the Internet had still not been restored and no repair date was scheduled. Kim had to take an author around to meet some editors for three days; so she wouldn't be in the office. During this time (we're now up to day 13 of the assistant's tenure) we needed a photocopy of the author's manuscript to bring to one of our appointments. The assistant quickly prepared a copy and handed it to Kim, who was dashing out of the door. At the meeting with the editor of *Organic Style*, Kim and the author realized that the pages of the manuscript were out-of-order and upside-down and that the chapter on organics was even missing. This was humiliating. Kim knew the author expected the mistake to be addressed immediately.

In our partnership each leans on the other for certain skills which she does not possess. Kim leans on Caitlin to have the tough conversations. She has a brilliant way of remaining calm and measured in the face of conflict. Kim tends to get emotional and overreact. Kim called Caitlin and couldn't reach her. But the author was standing there expecting a resolution. Kim called the assistant and asked her to rush a clean copy of the manuscript to the editor, because we had just left her office and had given her an incomplete version. When she began profusely apologizing, Kim very succinctly told her there was 'no reason to apologize, just please don't make that mistake again because a) it's embarrassing and b) it's unacceptable quality at our firm'. After the call, the author congratulated Kim for being firm but fair.

The following evening our assistant stopped by Kim's desk, asked to make a time to talk to her, and promptly burst into tears.

'What's wrong?' Kim asked. She thought she must have had a horrible personal problem, when in fact *we* had a horrible *personnel* problem. She went on to explain that she wanted to do a good job and be successful but she needed more. She needed positive reinforcement and support – much more support. Kim wasn't to tell her what she did wrong, but what she did right. She couldn't function if Kim continued to be so negative. She needed to applaud her efforts and gently point out where things could be done better. Kim was shocked. Not only had she completely misread the situation, she had been applauding her own management skills.

We've told this story countless times to other managers and the feedback falls firmly into two camps: the get-rid-of-her, she's too needy and her job as the team assistant is to worry about the team and not herself; and the good-for-her, she told you what kind of management style she needs.

It was a management lesson for us. After a few days of soul-searching, we realized that we had a good employee and should do everything we could to try to train her and keep her. If someone is smart and a hard-worker, then they are worth any extra effort management needs to expend to help them do their jobs more effectively.

Situational leadership: Taking charge

All of the women we interviewed had their own unique philosophies and approach to leadership. The model that works well for many women, including us, is an approach called 'situational leadership'. Situational leadership is being the right girl in the right place at the right time. Most women do this every day: they try not to get angry with a nervous colleague on their first day; they keep a close eye on some staff because they need more supervision; or give lots of latitude to those who can handle the freedom.

Our favorite management guru, Ken Blanchard, author of the *One Minute Manager* (HarperCollins, 2004) and the One Minute series, created a model for situational leadership in *Leadership and the One Minute Manager* (HarperCollins, 2004) that allows you to analyze the needs of the employee and adopt the most appropriate leadership style. It sounds complicated, but it's easy and makes perfect sense to us.

First, learn the four styles of Blanchard's leadership: directing, coaching, supporting, and delegating. When you're *directing*, you provide very specific direction and closely monitor progress towards the goal. When you're *coaching*, you continue to direct and closely monitor, but you also begin to explain decisions, solicit suggestions, and support progress. When you *support*, you facilitate and support the efforts towards accomplishing tasks as well as giving your subordinates responsibility for making their own decisions. Finally, when you're *delegating*, you turn over responsibility for decision making and problem solving to the individual.

Blanchard identifies four types of employees. He has given a little alphanumeric code for each one, which we find a bit boring and difficult to remember; so we've renamed them. Blanchard calls his 'low competence, high commitment' employees D1s. We call them 'young and eagers' and we wish we found more. The young and eagers are brand new to the workforce and know very little about the real world, yet possess an enormous amount of enthusiasm and desire to do a good job. Blanchard's D2s are 'low competence, low commitment', and we call these 'get rid of 'ems'. Life's too short to have people on the team who neither know what they're doing nor want to succeed. Blanchard's D3s exhibit 'moderate to high competence and variable commitment'. We call this group the 'competent but needies'; they know what they're doing and do it well, yet need regular encouragement and support. Finally the D4s exhibit 'high competence and high commitment' and they're our 'superstars'.

Now put it all together. *Direct **the young and eagers.*** Tell them in very clear terms what to do, how to do it, and when it needs to be done. Give the young and eagers systems – remember many of them have never worked before. Show them how to organize their desk, organize their work, and organize their time. Give them frequent reminders and systems for checking in – a daily to-do list in the morning and an afternoon what-got-done e-mail is a great way to keep them focused and working. We ask our assistant to do the agenda for our weekly staff meeting and then distribute the minutes. This task helps her learn our business, know what everyone is working on, and take ownership of keeping track of the team – three key pieces to her development.

If you find yourself with some **get rid of 'ems** on your team, and you have the energy to give them a chance, then *coach*. Give direction and feedback and support and praise to build their self-esteem, and then involve them in decision making to restore their commitment. Coaching can be difficult and, at the very least, time consuming. You're not just teaching the employee the responsibilities of his job, but trying to re-inspire him, too. If you are going to take this on, sit down with your employee and explain where things are going wrong. Be specific and direct. One of our most senior and trusted employees went through a bad time. She started coming in late every day, missing deadlines and meetings, and began acting inappropriately around other members of our team. We sat her down and laid down the law: while we cared about her and respected the work she had done for us in the past, her current performance was unacceptable and it had to change immediately or she would have to find another job. We're happy to report that she completely turned it around and has been a star ever since.

Support your **competent but needies.** They don't need you to tell them how to do their work; they just need encouragement and recognition for a job well done. Laurice Duffy, president of LDK Cleaning Service, has been running a cleaning business for ten years. In an industry where turnover is extremely high, she has had some of her crew since the day she started. The key to her success is communication. All of her employees can clean – well – however she wants them to know how important their work is to the business. After all, they are the heart of the operation and she treats them as such. She spends almost 50% of her time communicating with her crew (not always easy, because for most

English is not their first language). She has a morning 'meeting' when they come to pick up their supplies for the day. She reviews their schedule and points out any special instructions for specific clients. She checks in with them during the day, and her supervisors call her at the end of each shift, reviewing the day's jobs. Her girls, as she calls them, are all competent cleaners. However, they need to know that Laurice is paying attention to their work and that she appreciates all of their efforts.

If you're fortunate enough to find any *superstars* on your team, then *delegate* responsibilities and projects to them. They know what to do and how to do it, and don't relish you looking over their shoulder. They should be recognized for their accomplishments and promoted through the ranks. Superstars are rare and won't stay around unless you make their career development your priority. Engage them in their work process. Do they want a weekly update meeting with you? A daily e-mail? A monthly check-in? A combination of the above? Let them set the schedule and come to you when they need to.

Remember that your best people will work through these stages of development and that, if you give someone new responsibilities, they may be working at a different level in those areas while continuing to excel in the parts of their job in which they have more experience.

The Word: Libby Sartain, Chief of People, Yahoo!

Libby Sartain is senior vice president, Human Resources and chief of people, Yahoo!. With more than 25 years of experience in human resource management, Libby is responsible for leading Yahoo! Inc.'s global human resources efforts and for managing and developing the human resources team. She also focuses on attracting, retaining, and developing employees who will promote and strengthen the company culture as well as represent the powerful Yahoo! brand.

Prior to joining Yahoo! in August 2001, Libby Sartain was 'vice president of people' at Southwest Airlines, where she had been an employee since 1988. She managed a staff of 300 and led all the human resources activities at the airline, including employment, training, benefits, and compensation. She also played a key role in developing an employment strategy, which helped to double employee growth in six years.

Libby shared her thoughts on leadership, women in the workplace, balancing work and career development and family.

- I believe you serve those you lead by giving them the tools, knowledge, and mentorship they need to get their job done. Forming good relationships above you, on the same level with you, and below you is how people succeed in the workplace. This is accomplished by thinking about what others need, not what you need.
- I'm nice *and* I have a corner office. The challenges that women face in the workplace are different from what I faced almost 30 years ago. My group's challenge was that we were the first generation of women who actually had the same goals and dreams for their careers as men, and we walked right into the 'old boys' network'. Today's generation of women (and I am speaking about this not only as a human resources executive, but as the mother of a 22-year-old woman) are faced with a different reality. The law schools, the MBA programmes, and the med schools are all fifty-fifty, women and men. So when 'it' [gender differences in the workplace] comes at them, they don't recognize

it and are completely blind-sided. I think as time goes on, 'it' will become less and less of an issue.

- Some of the problems stem from attitude and outlook. Don't look for discrimination from bosses, peers, co-workers, and subordinates. As you go up the rungs, sometimes you need to be a little quieter and listen and learn. When situations arise, I ask myself if it was because I am a woman, but generally I see the same challenges for men at the highest levels. People always point to the absence of women CEOs as proof that women are discriminated against in the workplace. I have a different view. I think of all the senior executive women I know, I don't know too many who want to be CEOs. I think that women who have children realize that being a CEO is often too much to take on.

- Women and men have the same hopes and dreams coming into the workplace. Most people come to work every day wanting to give their best, and to give value and add value. And they want to know what, if they deliver what is expected of them, they will get in return.

Be Honest: Your Strengths and Weaknesses As a Leader

According to Hay's study, trust and confidence in top leadership was the single most reliable predictor of employee satisfaction in an organization. So, to keep happy and productive people, you must continually evaluate your strengths and weaknesses as a leader. We used the findings from the study to create the following checklist:

- Do you communicate the company's overall business strategy to employees? Make sure each department knows how their goals move the entire operation forward. It's important for senior managers to interact with all levels of the operation. Employees need to feel part of the bigger goal of an organization, otherwise they are easily distracted and become uninterested in their tasks. This is especially true of new members of the workforce who have a number separate tasks rather than entire projects to accomplish.

- Do you communicate how the employees' contributions help to achieve key business objectives? Employees want constant communication, especially about how their efforts help the organization to succeed. Create systems for communicating good news to individuals, departments and the entire company. Many large corporations have established company intranet sites for intra-company communication. Information is shared between departments, and employees are even encouraged to blog about their activities.

- Do you share information on both how the company is doing and how an employee's own division is doing? Employees, especially ones who own company stock as part of their retirement or pension plans, have a vested interest in the company's success and want regular reports.

- Do you know your own job inside and out and have a solid familiarity with your employees' tasks? As a manager you have a responsibility to lead by example.

- Do you search for ways to guide your organization to new heights? One of the leader's most important roles is to move the business to the next level.

- When things go wrong, do you analyze the situation, fix it and move on to the next challenge, avoiding placing the blame on others or holding on to past issues? Placing blame is the fastest way to lose the confidence of the team. We've heard it again and again in our interviews – bad bosses are blamers. The number two no-no, by the way, is taking credit for the team's work. As the leader you need to take pride in the accomplishments of your team. After all, if they succeed, you succeed.

- Do you make sound and timely decisions, ensuring that your staff can meet their deadlines? The worst thing you can do is hold the team up because you are too busy to give timely feedback.
- Are you a good role model for your employees? You can't just tell them what to do; they must see you doing. Of course, there is a flip-side to this too; they had better not see you acting badly, either.
- Do you care about your employees' well-being and job satisfaction? You'd better.
- Do you work with your team to develop good working habits and a sense of responsibility? Don't take for granted that the team understands what ownership of a task means.
- Do you make sure that subordinates understand what they are supposed to accomplish and know how to get the tasks done? Subordinates need the big picture and the nitty gritty. Don't overlook that.
- Do you operate as a team and not just a collection of individuals doing their respective jobs? Truly operating as a team takes time and effort. Managers need to evaluate the strengths and weaknesses of each team member, and then work out a game plan to get the most productivity from the group.

Are You Using the Full Capabilities of Your Organization?

According to Meredith Belbin, author of *Management Teams: Why They Succeed or Fail* (Butterworth-Heinemann, 2003), there are nine team roles, and we all carry out one function or more. The key to a good, efficient team is to create a healthy balance of these individuals or to identify the roles that you need your team members to play, even if that's not their natural role.

Belbin's nine team roles are as follows.

Plant
Original thinkers; they generate new ideas; they offer solutions to problems; they think in radically different ways, laterally, imaginatively.

Resource Investigator
They are creative; they like to take ideas and run with them; they are extrovert and popular.

Coordinator
They are highly disciplined and controlled; they can focus on objectives; they unify a team.

Shaper
Very achievement orientated, they like to be challenged and get results.

Monitor Evaluator
They are calm and detached; they are objective thinkers, who analyze and balance and weigh.

Team Worker
Supportive and cooperative, they make good diplomats, because they want only what is best for the team.

Implementer
With good organizational skills, they display common sense and they like to get the job done.

Completer
They check details; they tidy up after themselves; they are painstakingly conscientious.

Specialist
Dedicated to acquiring a specialized skill, they are extremely professional and have drive and dedication.

At YC Media, we look for *shapers*. We need highly motivated publicists who want to achieve results. We also need them to exhibit *completer* skills, and so we have created systems that force the shapers to 'sweat the details'.

The Mistakes Women Make: Sometimes It's Harder Being a Girl

Is there a woman manager whom you really admire, a boss who has always been supportive and fair, shepherding you through every step of your career, teaching, coaching, and then promoting you up the ranks? We didn't have one either. Excellent bosses are rare, and excellent female bosses are rarer still. We're not selling out the sisterhood here. There's a double-standard in the workplace. What's okay for a man is most definitely not okay for a woman. Over and over in our interviews we heard the same thing: 'I'd much rather work for a man; women are too emotional.' Sarilee Norton, president of Tru-Tech Business for Temple Inland summed it up best, 'A man can rant and rave and they say he's angry. A woman can rant and rave and they say she's crazy. If they can dismiss you as crazy, they don't have to pay attention to the issue.'

Try to identify a role model in your company and follow in her footsteps. We've had bosses who were obviously brilliant, creative, and talented people. They ran teams, small and large, and we wanted to work hard for them each day. Yet, even with all of their obvious talents and successes, we always felt they could have done more to inspire and support their staff. After spending just a couple of hours on the Internet researching leadership training for women, we were shocked to find that most of the female mentors, or even virtual mentors, were older, white women wearing sensible shoes and suits. The advice they offer to young women going to their first job interview sounds like bad Emily Post: 'When you meet someone new, a first impression is made in the first 30 seconds. You'll want to pay attention to everything you can control in those 30 seconds, such as your attire, poise, etiquette, eye contact, voice, and handshake. Try to convey professionalism and warmth. As for your attire, remember that dressing for success never goes out of style! Stand tall, and always shake hands and introduce yourself. Make your handshake a complete and firm grip. Be sure to maintain eye contact (as opposed to gazing at the door or the ceiling, which can happen when you're nervous). Looking people in the eye conveys confidence and openness. Pay attention to how you sit in a chair, how you cross your legs (at the ankle is best, if at all), and how you hold your hands (in your lap). Your poise is part of your package. How is your voice? A soft voice makes others have to work too hard to listen. On the other hand, a loud voice can come on too strong. Many people lower or speed up their voices when they are anxious. Be aware of your tendencies.'

Is she kidding? 'Your poise is part of your package.' We stopped listening right there. Of course your poise is important, but would you say it that way? Were our mothers and grandmothers fighting for us to go to university and get jobs we enjoy just so we could be forced into sensible shoes and nylon business suits? We hope not. Nothing about that conveys leadership. Our vision of leadership allows individuals to be themselves while working for the greater good of the group. Of course, a corporate culture comes into play, but it should be possible to be a good leader and still maintain your own identity.

Leader, Know Thyself: Personality Traits and Tests

No one would describe us as company girls; so, when the women we interviewed presented us with corporate jargon and acronyms, we did some homework. We found that personality tests are widely given in job interviews, career counselling centres, and at management training seminars. The results are supposed to help you to know yourself better so you can flex your management style in order to deal with different personalities. You're taught to adapt your style as different situations require. We were generally sceptical of this kind of thing until one of our colleagues told us a story. An executive at a fast-growing company, she was feeling overwhelmed with the management challenges that her expanding staff presented. She requested some management training and was sent off site to a one-day seminar. Upon entering the seminar, the group was given the Myers-Briggs Type Indicator. Developed by Katherine Briggs and her daughter Isabel Briggs Myers and based on Swiss psychologist Carl Gustav Jung's studies on psychological type, the MBTI scale is made up of four basic categories, each of which has two opposite poles. People generally lean towards one pole or the other, either moderately or, in some cases, quite strongly. From this fundamental division, eight psychological 'preferences' and 16 personality 'types' emerge. Management consultants use the test results to predict behaviour. For example, extremely extrovert people have to understand that, when an introvert member of their team doesn't stand up and cheer for a job well done, they are not being disrespectful; they are just not comfortable standing up and cheering. For a free personality test online, visit www.businessballs.com.

Extraversion-Introversion

The first preferences relate to how we deal with the outside world. Extraverts (E) are energized by having interactions with others and may often speak without thinking something through. They are people of action and present their best abilities to the world. Introverts (I) prefer quiet reflection and may think about something and never get to the point of telling others. They keep their best skills to themselves and present their secondary skills to others.

Sensing-Intuition

The next set of preferences, sensing-intuition, differences affect how we take in and process data. Sensors (S) gather information through experiences and are practical and orderly. Intuitors (N) gather information through relationships and concepts, picking things up by watching and grasping ideas before getting to grips with the detail.

Thinking-Feeling

The thinking-feeling differences affect how we make decisions. Thinkers (T) make decisions objectively and impersonally, using logic. Feelers (F) make decisions subjectively and personally, based on what they feel is 'right'. A thinker will tend to decide things based on logic, while a feeler will base it more on their emotions and the feelings of others. It is interesting that, in the United States at least, about 67% of all men are thinkers, while 67% of females are feelers.

Judging-Perceiving

Finally, judging-perceiving differences affect how we prefer to live. Judgers (J) like being planned and structured and having things settled and decided. Perceivers (P) like being spontaneous, unstructured, open, and flexible.

It all sounds too complicated until we return to our friend's management training class. After the trainees answered a series of questions, the results were scored and the group was divided into judgers and perceivers and asked to plan a holiday.

The perceivers chose a tropical island vacation and filled their days with activities and their nights with social events. Each day was chock full of options for fun and relaxation. They neglected, however, to choose a date or to plan how they were to get to their destination. The judgers in contrast decided when they were going and how they were getting there, right down to airport transfers, but neglected to choose a place where they wanted to be. Amazing!

Two groups of similarly successful professionals with diametrically opposite views of the world. What became apparent to them (and us) was that, if you have an indication of a person's traits, you can support their natural weaknesses. Another colleague, Amie Malkin, the managing director of healthcare for Burson-Marsteller in London, is an ESTJ, an extravert, practical, objective, and structured person. Her reviews most commonly recommend that she offer 'more carrot, less stick'. For her, knowing this about herself has enabled her to have more patience with people and to be more supportive and less directive.

To check this out for ourselves, we went online and took a free personality test (www.ustechnicaljobs.com). Here's what it said:

Kim scored as an ENFP (extravert, intuitive, feeler, perceiver). ENFPs tend to be: enthusiastic, talkative, and outgoing; clever, curious, and playful; deeply caring, sensitive, and gentle; highly innovative, creative, and optimistic; adaptable and resourceful, but sometimes disorganized. The most important thing to ENFPs is freedom to see possibilities, make connections, and be with a variety of people.

Caitlin is an ISFJ (introvert, sensor, feeler, judger). ISFJs tend to be cautious, gentle, and thoughtful; hesitant until they know people well, then affectionate and caring; very literal and aware of the physical world; uncompromising about personal standards and easily offended; diligent and conscientious, organized and decisive. The most important thing to ISFJs is living a stable, predictable life and helping people in real ways.

Clearly the quiz has deemed us total opposites, but in such a way that our personalities are complementary and in fact beneficial to our working relationship. For instance, Kim's ability to be continually outgoing and talkative enables her to keep up with the busy social aspect of running a PR firm, and Caitlin's receptive and thoughtful nature positions her well to manage the team and deal with sensitive situations. In our case, the sum is most definitely greater than the two parts.

Girl Talk: Courtney Lynch and Angela Morgan

Courtney Lynch and Angela Morgan are founders of Lead Star, a leadership training company that presents dynamic, energetic workshops which focus on discovering and developing the natural leadership traits women possess. On their website (www.leadingfromthefront.com), Courtney and Angela describe themselves in terms of their roles: Courtney as a 'leader, wife, daughter, friend and lawyer'; and Angie as a 'leader, wife, mother, volunteer and employee'. One role missing in their descriptions was marine. Both joined the U.S. Marine Corps while at university in the ROTC (Reserve Officer Training Corp) programme. They graduated as officers and, at the ages of 22 and 23, respectively, began their service commanding platoons of 50 soldiers. Both on the way they lead their lives and on the lessons they teach, the Marine Corps has had a profound impact. It is their belief that leadership skills can be used in all of the roles women play in their lives: a stay-at-home mother needs leadership skills to calm the chaos; a daughter needs leadership skills to care for an ageing parent; and a manager needs leadership skills to get a good result from their team. At Lead Star, they define a leader as one who influences outcomes and inspires others. We spoke to them about their leadership training and their philosophy, 'Lead as you are. Always'.

How did being in the Marine Corps prepare you to be great leaders and train others on leadership?
The Marine Corps gave us all the tools we needed to lead – from practical leadership principles and character traits to rigorous training in environments where we were

encouraged to succeed, but where failure as we developed was allowed. Thus, once we got to the 'real world', we were proven leaders. The Marine Corps has been training leaders for 230 years. Their methods have withstood the test of time. In the Marine Corps and at Lead Star, leadership is not about being complex, it's about being effective. Not only did the Marine Corps give us great training, it gave us great opportunities to apply the skills we learned. Our leadership skills focused on taking care of others, and as Marine officers we were immediately tasked with that. In the private sector it would take many years to achieve that level of management/leadership experience.

Do you think there are differences between the skills needed for great women leaders v. men leaders?
Strong leadership skills transcend gender. All leaders must have integrity, take initiative, have sound judgment, and take care of those they lead. While the skills are the same, leadership styles are personal and individualized. We all have different strengths and weaknesses (and some may be compatible with our gender), but regardless we have to recognize them and overcome them in our efforts to be the best leader possible.

Studies have shown that to be effective leaders, women and men have to lead differently. Was this your experience in the Marine Corps? If so can you describe the differences?
We think every individual needs to lead differently. Women don't need to take on masculine personas to be strong leaders. We learned this early on. One of our few female officers (1,000 out of 180,000 Marines are female officers) was a very nice woman with an odd quirk. Whenever she

was in front of her troops or in front of men, she adopted a manly persona. She lowered her voice, changed her posture and ultimately forfeited her credibility. She also recommended to me [Courtney] that if I wanted to succeed in the Marine Corps, I would have to do the same. I was torn. As this was the commanding officer, I was supposed to follow her orders, and, while I appreciated that she was trying to help me, I strongly disagreed with her. Ironically enough, what saved me was a crusty old Colonel, a stereotypical marine. He called me into his office and, without acknowledging what was happening with my commanding officer, he told me that I needed to lead as who I was. He said, 'Being a leader is not about playing a part, but being credible and being yourself, and, if you don't lead as you are, you will never earn the respect of those you command.'

The lesson we took with us from the Marine Corps is that, while good leaders share consistent traits, they exhibit them in many different ways. We've worked for great leaders who were shy, who were boisterous, who were stoic, and who were warm. Personality plays a big role in your leadership style.

What are the three most important traits (skills) women should learn to be great leaders?
Integrity, decisiveness, and courage. Courage to take risks, to make a change, and even to fail.

How do you manage to be a strong leader without being labelled a bitch?
The strongest leaders display compassion and a sense of service to others. Poor leaders get caught up in the kudos

of their position or the power and status a title brings. Those are the leaders who are likely to be labelled 'bitch', because they have defined leadership to mean something about them instead of about those they lead.

As a leader you must be confident. The easiest way to be confident is to be competent. The Marines taught us the importance of leading from the front. The Marines encourage you to continually take initiative. However, you must set standards that you can and do meet. When Courtney was a marine, she carried a 9 mm pistol. She had never touched a gun before joining the Marines and wasn't a particularly skilled shot. The marines in the platoon she commanded were required to qualify on a large rifle, an M-16 to be exact, and so she had to meet that standard also. It wasn't easy, but she did it. Leaders meet the standards they ask of others. In the private sector, an obvious example of leading from the front is with the 8 a.m. meeting. If the leader calls the meeting, then the leader needs to meet the standard and be there on time. Too often managers will call a 9 o'clock meeting and then saunter in at 9.15. It's disrespectful to the people who have been waiting for you, and it undermines your ability to lead.

We've found that as women we're not immediately accepted as leaders. How do we earn this critical buy-in?
Performance is the key to gaining buy-in and respect. Respect is what you should aspire to as a leader. You shouldn't strive to make people like you, but it is critical for them to respect you. We both agree that as women – or as any minority in an organization – you are likely to have to prove yourself more often than the majority, but, if you are a consistent performer, eventually your positive

reputation will build. As marines, we often felt responsibility for our entire gender. We weren't just acting as Courtney and Angie, but as women, and we took the responsibility seriously. We limited socializing with our marines to a minimum, and Courtney even adopted a policy of not going on dates with marines.

What do you think are the biggest leadership mistakes women make? What are the biggest mistakes that men make?
Women often confuse leadership with a popularity contest. Leading can be lonely. You are entrusted with responsibility and the opportunity to influence outcomes and inspire others. The need to make tough decisions for the good of the whole team often leads to dissatisfaction among individuals. Women tend to internalize this dissatisfaction more than they should. Accept the reality and move on.

Men struggle with compassion and communication skills more often than women. When you lack compassion you have a hard time anticipating the needs of your team and addressing them. This can ultimately hurt your efforts to build camaraderie and a sense of common purpose. Weak communication skills allow minor issues to become major issues.

Many women we interviewed have said that it is much easier for them to work for male bosses. Was this your experience in the Marine Corps, and do you have any thoughts on why this would be the case?
We have more experience with men in leadership roles. Yet, with the emphasis on leadership skills in the Corps, we almost became 'gender-blind'. Male or female became a moot point; we just recognized the positive differences of

working for leaders. When we've had a hard time working for a woman or a man it's probably because the person we are working for is not a leader. It's really not easier to work for a man. It's just easier to work for a leader.

How does leading from the front differ from other leadership styles?

Leaders who lead from the front continuously take the initiative and make decisions. They also meet or exceed the standards they expect others to meet. Leaders keep making decisions in order to keep making progress. The Corps taught us the '80% solution', that a good decision today is better than a great decision tomorrow. And procrastination is a decision all of its own.

There's so much conflicting information out there. Entire books are written on the premise that 'nice girls don't get promoted' or you can only 'win like a man'. How do we become strong, empowered, inspiring women without acting like men?

There is wide variety of information out there, but the heart of being an effective leader is understanding who you are and leading as you are. You've got to be credible in order to inspire others. That's why we started Lead Star. We wanted to inspire and empower women to lead as they are. We are proof positive that staying true to yourself is the key to being an authentic, capable leader. When you lead as you are you don't ignore your weaknesses - you always have to be working to improve - but you learn how to compensate for them with your strengths.

3

Team Building: You're Only As Good As Your Staff

One of the more non-negotiable facts of business life is that, in order to succeed as a leader, you need a solid team supporting you. Your employees are only as good as your selection and development of them; so, in addition to your overall goals, you need to always be focused on building and nurturing a team of hard workers you can trust and rely on.

Whether creating a team from scratch or supporting one that you've inherited, assembling the right mix of people is essential to the smooth operation of your company, team, division, or unit.

From hiring and training new members to winning the loyalty of the old-timers, we'll tell you what you need to know and do to create an environment in which team members – from assistants to associates – will flourish.

Evaluating Your Personnel: Do You Have the Team You Want?

Whether you hired them yourself, or they came with your new position, periodically you need to evaluate your team. Our preferred method of doing this is with an org (short for organizational) chart. An org chart is an illustration of the inner structure of a business or, in this case, your team. It is a presentation of the relationships within the team, identified by lines of authority. When you fill in your org chart with names and titles it makes it easy to visualize the inner structure of the group, and will make it easier to see holes in the staff or redundancies in responsibilities.

An org chart looks something like this.

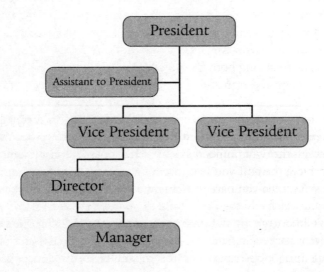

Create an org chart, listing the names of your employees and leaving space next to each name for the following information:

- title
- salary
- date of hire
- date of last review
- date of last rise
- date of last promotion

Answer the following questions as best you can for each employee:

- Is she expecting a rise and/or promotion?
- What are her responsibilities?
- Is she delegating correctly?
- Is she a good manager?
- Is she loyal to the company?
- Is she loyal to me?
- How is she feeling about her role in the company (happy, frustrated, anxious)?
- Is she following both the unspoken and spoken rules of the company and team?

Step back and, with your goals for the team in hand (increase sales/ generate publicity/design new products), ask yourself whether your team has the right number of people and the skills and the attitude to achieve them. If you have the right number of people but not the skills, then you have to think about retraining. If you have an attitude problem, then it is time to address it – and fast. If you don't have enough staff, then it is time to hire. If your boss is hesitant about adding to the payroll, get ready to make your case. Write up a job description, outline the reasons why it isn't possible for existing employees to fill the gap, and remember to demonstrate how this new hire is going to improve profitability down the road.

Telltale Signs that Your Employee May Be Getting Ready to Jump Ship

- Mysterious appointments during the day always alluded to in vague terms.
- Your Grateful Dead-loving assistant shows up for work dressed like a bank clerk.
- Every time you approach the printer, she rushes past you to snatch the pile of paper (CVs!) sitting in the tray.
- When you are within five feet of the employee's desk, she begins frantically closing Word documents.
- More than once a day you look out of the window and see your employee on the pavement, talking on her mobile phone.
- You can't quite put your finger on it, but your employee has developed a bit of a 'tude.
- When you assign a complex project to the employee, she doesn't ask follow-up questions.

The Right Fit: Making a Good Choice

So, based on the org chart and the goals you have been hired to achieve, do you have the people to get the job done? Once you're up to speed on the legalities of hiring (see page 55), then you can start looking. But whom do you hire? Where do you find them? How do you determine if they are right for you?

Who?

Before calling human resources or placing an ad, work out on paper what you need in an employee. This includes a list of desired skills, a salary range, and a rough idea of personality traits you think would mesh well with the existing group, especially the person to whom they will report. Also write out a complete job description so that you can articulate with accuracy what their daily, weekly, and monthly responsibilities will be.

Anat Baron, entrepreneur, reminds us that, while we might be looking for someone familiar, there are benefits to thinking broader. 'I am a big believer in diversity. Not just the normal ethnic/cultural kind, but diversity of ideas. I think teams work best when you mix people up – different backgrounds and work experience. They challenge each other. The common interest becomes getting the job done.'

Where?

If you've been promoted to a supervisory position in a company or corporation, your human resources department may have a policy of promoting from within or of handling the first stage of the recruitment process; so make HR your first stop.

If your business does not have an HR department, then it's up to you to get the word out. Depending on the level of the employee, you could take out an ad in the local paper, check in with career advisors at local colleges, register with websites such as Monster (www.monster.co.uk) or Careerbuilder (www.cbdr.co.uk), find a reputable headhunter by asking your colleagues or by checking the classifieds in a trade magazine, and/or e-mail people in your professional circle. Recently we sent an e-mail to our network asking for help finding an account executive (a mid-level associate in a public relations agency). Within days, our e-mail was disseminated to what seemed like hundreds of people and we began receiving CVs from friends, friends of friends, and friends of friends of friends. Since we were very specific about the skill set we sought, most of the referrals we received were legitimate candidates.

The one caveat worth noting about going to your personal network for job candidates is that, as we stated in our first book, you should stay away from considering or hiring friends, family, ex-bosses, ex-assistants, and ex-boyfriends or girlfriends. You want working relationships to be as baggage-free as possible.

How?

Interviewing, interviewing, and more interviewing – and trusting your gut. Even if HR sends you someone they've billed as the perfect candidate, if your instincts are signalling 'danger ahead', then approach with extreme caution. Ask lots of direct questions. Maybe even explain your concerns to a peer in the company and ask her to interview the person and give you a second opinion. It's our firm belief that if you sense a problem, there may well be one there, even if only in the chemistry between you and the potential employee.

Now, many people will tell you that you don't have to like an employee. If a quirky employee does an excellent job, then that should be enough. That may be true, if she works in the London office while you're in, say, Los Angeles, or if she's on the road most of the time. But, if you have to see this person and interact with her daily, or even weekly, it would make life a lot more pleasant if you liked her, too.

Stephanie Teuwen, president of Teuwen One Image, says, 'Once the skills have been established in the interview, then it's all about personality. It's a bit like dating! You need to get along well and be a team.' But don't hire someone just because you like them. About a year ago we were looking to hire a junior account executive to help us to run the office while learning the business. The ideal candidate would come with a little professional experience and a lot of enthusiasm for public relations. We interviewed a great person, who, on a personal level, we had a ton in common with. She was smart and fun to be around, but, when we asked her why she was interested in working for us, she said 'Because I figured it is time for me to have a real job.' While we liked her, we just couldn't trust that she 'got' what it meant to work in a professional office environment, and we didn't have the time or energy to bring her up to speed on the basics.

A Note for Entrepreneurs: Before You Hire

For those that own their own business hiring an employee is a very *big deal*. You are sometimes doubling your payroll with just one employee, and, when you double your company even on a small scale, the entire dynamic of your business changes. Before inviting someone to join the business, have the employee manual done, the payroll set up, the job responsibilities outlined, and most importantly work out for yourself the expectations you have for this employee. When you know exactly what you want and need from a new employee, you'll be able to communicate clearly from day one.

Legalities of Hiring

If there are holes that need to be filled and you run your own business, before you even think about calling a headhunter or taking out an ad, get some appropriate legal advice. Visit Business Link's website (www.businesslink.gov.uk) or the Department of Trade and Industry (www.dti.gov.uk), which offers a site map relating to aspects of employment relations.

Interviewing

When chatting with a potential candidate, keep in mind the spoken and unspoken rules of your work environment – the company culture – and share important details with candidates that you think have potential. Are there several out-of-town conferences that the employee will be expected to attend? Are the official office hours 9 to 5, but can most employees nonetheless be found at their desks at 6 or 7 o'clock at night? If there is an expectation of long hours, it is only fair to prepare the candidate. Also factor in the 'personality' of the office. Let's say that your group is highly productive, but conservative and relatively humourless; in that case, it might not be fair to anyone if you hired a high-energy, highly strung, arty candidate. Stephanie Teuwen says, 'Aside from figuring out if the potential employee has the required skills or transferable skills, my number one priority is their personality. Will they fit in our environment, be happy, complement the team, and enjoy our clients? I really try to see their soul and their heart without asking inappropriate questions. When I feel that the person is a potential "go", I have him or her meet the rest of the team for a casual discussion, and we regroup the following day to share our experience. Nobody would be hired if my team didn't like them. We're like a small family; we need to "adopt" the new member together.'

Ask yourself if you think a potential employee would be happy as a part of the group. It might be difficult for you yourself to make this judgement, especially if the candidate is keen to get the job; so consider setting up interviews with a few key team members, including her direct report.

Be honest about the job and the amount of grunt work required. You don't want new recruits baulking every time they are asked to file a piece of paper. If they are a newbie to your industry, and the reality is that they will be spending the first couple of years running errands, do them a favour and tell it like it is. We have had people turn our job offer down because they didn't like hearing that we were going to ask them to stuff a lot of gift bags. Of course it was a drag to keep interviewing, but it would have been a bigger drag to work with a bitter assistant.

If the candidate is between jobs, this is a perfect opportunity for you to test one another out. Bring them in for a week to work with you and the rest of the team. You won't learn everything about them in five days, but you should be witness to their highest quality of work as they try to win the job. If their best isn't good enough for you, then at least you will have found that out before you made them an offer.

No Mind Games and Power Trips During the Interview, Please

Do you know when you won't learn a single thing about a potential candidate? When you are treating the interview as an opportunity to play *big bad boss*. When Leigh Ann, a friend of ours, arrived at a public relations company for an internship interview, she was shown to an empty office with a single desk and a single chair. The owner came in and placed a pen on the table. She then handed her a piece of paper and a pencil, saying 'I want you to write a paragraph that will inspire a journalist to write about this pen.' When she returned and picked up the 'test', she shook her head and said 'Absolutely wrong.' She went on to explain that our friend was supposed to 'sell' the pen to journalists, something a final year undergraduate with no experience in public relations would never have known. Bottom line – it didn't make sense, and only served to make the candidate feel inferior and clam up.

To learn the most from potential candidates, make them feel comfortable. Remember to smile when you greet them, ask them if they found the office okay, offer them water, and spend the first few minutes chatting. Before jumping in on the tough questions, start with the lighter ones. You might ask a school-leaver what their favourite subject was at school or a more senior candidate how they found themselves in the industry. But don't start off an interview with a question about why they left their last job. The point is not to challenge them straightaway, or they'll be in defensive mode throughout the interview.

If You Teach Them: How to Train Effectively

Wouldn't it be a perfect world if you could just tell someone what needs to get done and never give it another thought? Or better still, if you didn't have to say anything at all, because your employee had ESP and was a self-starting perfectionist. Alas, the chances that you will lead a training-free existence are just about zero, and in fact training is one of the most important requirements of your job.

Everyone seems to agree that the most effective way to train is to make taking the time to do it right a priority and to recognize that you need to give the individuals on your staff different levels of guidance and different types of management (see situation leadership style, as discussed in Chapter 2). Junior staff members are still developing into professionals and so need your help cultivating the basics of office etiquette, as well as the nuts and bolts to actually perform their duties. Senior people shouldn't need to be schooled in the basics of professionalism or how to do their job, but they do need you to explain your vision and what their role in attaining it is.

Adrienne Arsht, chairman of the Board of TotalBank in Miami, recommends setting up the ground rules early with new senior employees: 'I would sit down and talk directly about your own management style: "This is what I mean when I say this or that. I respect you, that's why I hired you; so, if I come off rude, it isn't personal. When you hear something you don't like, come and talk to me about it directly."'

With both junior and senior staff members, consider establishing a mentor system among your team. Develop a few people on all levels to become mentors for all new employees. They need to know the company inside and out, be enthusiastic about being there, work well with you, and be a positive spokesperson for both the company and you. When a junior-level employee starts, partner them up with a peer who will answer their questions about the office (Where do I find pens? What is the policy on lunch? Where is the nearest bank?).

The early stage of training an employee is a delicate and crucial time. You need to teach them to take responsibility for their work and themselves, while showing that you are supportive. Tammy Blake, a senior manager at a publishing house, told us about scheduling a first day for new employees that will at least point them in the direction of achieving success at your company.

Sample first day plan

- Coffee with you (and new employee's direct report if that *isn't* you)
- Introduction to team mentor
- Team mentor brings new employee round the company for casual introductions
- Lunch with team mentor
- Afternoon with direct report to go over coming week's schedule

Your Gal Friday: Do You Need a Personal Assistant and What Should She Be Like?

Your personal assistant, almost more than any other member of your team, represents you to the outside world. In many cases, she is the first person that your professional network encounters en route to seeing you. Because she usually answers your phone and greets your guests, you want this assistant to shine. We know a very famous chef in our circle who had a wonderful PA. She was always responsive, pleasant, and professional. She knew where the chef was at all times and was able to get answers, confirm VIP reservations, and set up photo shoots on a quick turnaround. When she moved on, this chef hired a new assistant who did none of the above. Because, like most niche industries, the food world is so tiny, everyone was talking about this hiring blunder. Jokes were made, media opportunities were lost (because she couldn't or wouldn't get answers fast enough), and eventually she lost her job. And the chef? He lost a lot of face. What's the lesson here? Take a long hard look at your current assistant. Are you comfortable having her speak for you? Ask a few outside colleagues for a candid appraisal of what their experience with your assistant has been like.

If you're recruiting a PA, make sure you have enough work to fill his or her day. Unlike other staff positions, that of personal assistant is almost entirely dependent on you to assign tasks and responsibilities on a more or less daily basis. When you interview candidates, make sure there is a rapport, that they exude confidence, dress appropriately, and are polite. Avoid the pit bulls; they really don't make you look good, even if they can block your doorway to unwelcome guests. Hire someone that has shown loyalty to other bosses, because you don't want your PA to become the source of office gossip; if the assistant is disloyal to you, or not very professional, she will tell the staff if you are having problems with your husband, when you leave early, and whenever you are called upstairs. You can assess loyalty during the interview by asking candidates the best and worst things about their previous manager. Look at the CVs to see how long they kept each job and whether they listed any of their direct reports as references. And remember what Patty LaBelle told Caitlin as they were boarding a plane together during a book tour: your PA must 'always, always, always, represent'.

Good Witch or Big Bitch?

Here's a story from our friend Amy Curry.

A really good witch

My best female boss, Jackie, was someone who over the course of our working relationship managed to help me to develop self confidence, in which I was sorely lacking. She did this without the intention of mentoring or changing me. It was mostly an outcome of who she was as a boss and a person.

In thinking back, I guess the reasons for it working so well for me came down to several things, including:

- her belief that everyone in her team had something valuable to offer (hierarchy wasn't important; ideas were)
- her ability to delegate responsibilities and her trust that the task would get done
- her lack of need to micromanage
- her personality

She managed to pull together a team that had complementary skills so that everyone had their own responsibilities and domain. She respected everyone's opinions and encouraged ideas. Remarkably, she did not take disagreements as a sign of disrespect. Instead she saw them as commitment to the idea and passion for the project. She and I would often have heated discussions about the work we were involved in, and, through them, we learned a tremendous amount from each other and were able to arrive at some conclusion. Nothing was taken personally, because the discussion really focused on articulating ideas and trying to see whose background and power of persuasion were most able to move the ideas forward.

In my case being valued for what I could do and being given responsibilities was truly important. Mostly, the fact that she appreciated my work and was not threatened by it (because she and I had a very different professional backgrounds and skills) was liberating. Although there was a structure – she was the PI (principle investigator of the project) and I was eventually promoted to project manager – what worked best for me was the fact that there was less formal hierarchy in the working environment.

Finally, Jackie had no interest in micromanaging the project, which meant that we would check in about our workload and deadlines and discuss what our plans for completing the work were, but then how and when we did it was up to us. This more flexible type of goal setting works well for me. It implies trust: I say I am going to get something done, my boss trusts that I will, and doesn't therefore manage the little steps to getting there.

All these things are critical, but I think most critical to the success of this working relationship was the way in which our personalities and work styles matched. Though we don't work together any more, we still meet for lunch as friends. We had a natural connection in style and outlook.

Amy's boss Jackie was a Good Witch certainly. She seems to have done everything right, starting with the golden rule of management: respect your people and respect yourself. She demonstrated respect by encouraging ideas and soliciting input and opinions. She had faith in their abilities by stepping back and not micromanaging. She took her ego out of it and focused on moving ideas forward. Wow!

Handling Old Loyalties:
Was Your Predecessor Cooler Than You?

It is scary to inherit an employee, let alone a whole team. Think about when a new manager was hired over you. What emotions did it bring up? You were probably anxious that she would want to replace you; resentful that you had to prove yourself all over again; distrustful of the direction she was going to take the group; unsettled by the change; defensive about your contribution and your right to be there; and even nostalgic about the way things used to be. And, let's be honest, there might even have been a small part of you that wanted to see her fail.

Now turn it around: this is the emotional landscape that you are now managing. If truth be told, you have to prove yourself worthy of your team's loyalty, hard work, and respect. This is even more challenging if your predecessor was adored. Everyone we interviewed said the same thing, 'Take it slowly.' Unless you have an employee who is blatantly undermining you, try not to fire anyone right away. You want to spend the first few weeks watching and listening. Here is a trick: assess the team you have been given and identify the leader in the group. This is the person that inspires those around them (even at a junior level) and that many turn to with questions. This is someone you want on your side. Beware of the ones that are most solicitous; they are not who you need right now. You need the corporate equivalent of the trendsetter. You want them to make respecting and listening to you the latest trend. If they are not on your side, then make it your mission to turn it around. Because of their power in the group, they can undermine your authority.

People are going to fear you, so use this to your advantage by maintaining a professional distance. (Don't go out to lunch with the team unless you initiate it, avoid the water cooler chit chat, skip the drinks after work.) And don't fall into the trap of wanting everyone to like you. Unfortunately it seems as though women have more challenges in this area than men. Beth Kramer, a VP of New Product Development, tells us, 'I think the biggest problem with employees I inherited is they didn't see the need to listen to me or pay attention – there were gender issues here, and also issues around differences in academic degrees and work experience. Because our organization was strongly collaborative and consensus driven, I couldn't simply say, "Because I said so."'

If your team wasn't prepared for your arrival or promotion, it can also make for a rocky transition, as was the case when Ayelet Baron was hired: 'The first challenge was they were not told about the changes by their management team until the last minute. And when they were told about it, the vision for the change was never shared with them, so we started off with a very tense environment. They had lost their trust in management looking out for their needs and were suspicious of the new management.' To make things worse for Ayelet, 'When I asked the former manager about the performance of each person on his team (I didn't know most of them), he failed to mention that one of them got a poor rating on his last review. And when I inherited this group of people, I found out that most of the internal clients didn't want him working on their projects. Everyone on the team liked him but knew that he was the weakest link. I had to spend a lot of time giving him a new assignment and working closely on performance expectations. This took a lot of time and energy away from forming the new team.'

So what to do? Step back, evaluate your team, and be very clear about who you are and what you have been hired to do. A great opportunity to do this is during the one-to-one meetings you are going to set up with your senior team members. Show that you want to do whatever you can to help them to succeed in their careers, outline the vision you have been given for the company, and, whatever you do, don't start the discussion by introducing sweeping changes. Remember that the most successful transitions are those that begin and end with honesty.

We know that inheriting a team, whether of people you know or strangers, is scary, but, for the good of the team, fake it until you feel it – confidence, that is.

The Word: Dianne Nolan, Coach

Dianne Nolan, women's basketball head coach at Fairfield University, Connecticut, has been responsible for recruiting and coaching. As one of the country's best coaches, she has a lot to say about making a team work as one. She shares her tips and experiences with us below.

What do you do when players are not acting like members of a team?
I have an open door policy and the players know that when they are in my office and I close the door the following discussion is important and confidential. I will close the door and address the issue with the player. I will cite specific examples of behaviour that lead me to believe the team is not coming first in the player's mind. I ask the player to explain her actions. After listening, I will outline steps to take so that she can improve her behaviour and begin to show her support of team goals.

How do you get the players to work together?
I gather the team together and share an outline of team expectations and goals. I ask for their input. Together we map out a strategy to accomplish the team goal. Daily reminders of the goal are reinforced with signs in the locker room and notes in their lockers, and we have a cheer following practice – yelling out the goal together. Each player fully understands the mission of the team.

How long does it take for a team to gel?
It varies. Every team has its own personality. Each year players mature and graduate and new players join the

team. Communication and energy are essential. You must exercise patience and understanding and use the senior members to help the younger players feel comfortable within the team. Each player needs to know their role and how important that role is in accomplishing the team goal. I try to blend the team quickly by sending members on a scavenger hunt through campus. I divide the team into groups of three. This one-hour exercise has paid enormous dividends in team bonding.

Thoughts about how to integrate a new player into an existing team?
When a player is in their comfort zone they perform to the best of their ability. I learn as much as I can about the player through non-threatening activities. I need to understand what makes them tick in pressure situations. I set up projects and spend time with each player while she is involved in the project. I access each player's personality and coach them accordingly. I have found you must treat each player fairly, but often not the same. They are individuals operating in a team setting.

What do you look for when recruiting players?
Talent, talent, talent. I want players who will help us to win ball games, possess the academic credentials to succeed in the classroom, have a strong work ethic, and are good citizens. Playing Division 1 Basketball is challenging, and I look for players who embrace the challenge. They need to be headstrong, have passion, loyalty, and discipline. A good sense of humour is helpful!

Do you have any thoughts about coaching new team members?
Get to know them as quickly as possible. Find out about
their family background, their academic history, and their
likes and dislikes. The more I really know them, the better
I can mesh them with the group. Getting them into a
comfort zone is paramount.

*What challenges did you face when you took over as coach
(regarding acceptance from the players)?*
I was the first full-time female coach hired at Fairfield.
Every day was a challenge. I had to start from scratch. My
first day, I was handed a key to an office with a steel grey
desk and nothing in it. I was young and determined.
Sometimes ignorance is bliss! I met with the team as soon
as possible, outlined my expectations, and away we went.
The players were super. Their previous year was not
successful, and they wanted to be winners. I conveyed that
nothing is free and we were going to out-work everyone.
They bought into the system and worked hard.

How did you earn their respect?
Knowing your craft is so important. If you are going to lead
people, you had better have a firm grasp of the discipline.
Exercising understanding, patience and having energy and
self-confidence are important leadership traits. Staying true to
your word gains immediate respect. I told the players we were
going to work hard, and we did. The practices were planned
by the minute and were physically and mentally challenging.
We worked in the weight room and had rules for campus
behaviour. Early in my career, after a victory and team
celebration at dinner, the players were issued a curfew, since
the game was on the road. Later in the evening, in the ladies

room, I met two of our star players washing their hands. It was well after curfew. The next game was our opening home tournament, as you can imagine, a very popular event. I suspended the two players and demonstrated to team that I was true to my word. Respect is earned.

Tips for building an effective team?
Surround yourself with good people. People, who are talented, have energy, a good work ethic, integrity, and passion. Do your best when your best is expected.

What Do They Want from Me?

The chances are that you have at some point been an employee. In fact, unless you own the company, you probably still report to someone. To find out what your people need from you, step back and ask yourself what you need or needed from your higher-ups. Even better, ask yourself what you didn't get and really could have used more of.

Your employees need a lot from you. Here are some of the key things you should be ready, willing, and able to provide.

1. **Clear vision.** You should tell them where the company is going, what their career prospects are, and how you see the team working together.

2. **Support.** In every sense of the word, including emotional support (where it pertains to business goals), technical support, logistical support, and staff support to help to get their job done.

3. **Respect:** For their work, for them as individuals, for their contribution to the organization.

4. **Feedback:** We hesitate to say that you are a parental figure, but unfortunately that is the case. At the very least you are an authority figure for your employees, so they are looking to you for feedback on their work. We had an assistant who needed and even asked us for feedback every day. Certainly we were busy, but it would make her happy and more productive if we spent a few minutes talking with her.

5. **Answers:** They are looking to you to be available for answers on a wide range of subjects. Or at least to help them with finding the solution.

6. **Freedom:** One of the best bosses we spoke to, Christine Deussen, president and founder of Deussen Global Communications, Inc., believes, 'Most of all, I think employees need freedom. Freedom to grow and stretch, freedom to make their own mistakes, freedom to try out new ideas. We all continually learn from each other, and, if people feel stymied, we will not see their creative best. I am always there as a resource, and of course I will always check up on things until I am comfortable that the work they are putting out is up to our company's standards, but they need to be free to get to the end product in their own way.'

Shifting Employee Expectations

There are needs that your employees will expect you to fulfil that you just will not, and should not, be able to. Kathleen Hutchenson, a senior editor at a magazine, had an employee who said she wanted to be Kathleen's friend. Kathleen ran a casual and fun team, but that didn't mean that she could befriend the employees. Abigail Disney, founder and president of the Daphne Foundation, shares this: 'I learned the hard way that you cannot get too close to people's personal problems when you manage them. Even though you really care about and have compassion for the people you work with, getting too much in the middle of their life's problems can compromise the integrity of the dynamic between you; so it is better to express respect and compassion for them, but to observe and respect their privacy and autonomy at all times.'

When you have an employee that makes an impossible request of you, it is a good opportunity to look objectively at what you are projecting to your staff. In your new mode of clear communication, be direct about what you are defining as appropriate. In Kathleen's case she was put in the uncomfortable position of having to tell her employee that, while she liked her and enjoyed their working relationship, she had made it a policy not to socialize with employees. If you are not clear with your employees about what is and isn't acceptable to you, you might put yourself in the position of being taken advantage of.

How to Tell If You're Being Taken Advantage Of
Your deadlines aren't the priority for your employees

As the leader of the team, the deadlines you set for projects need to take precedence over all other tasks. The assumption made by your employees should be that you don't arbitrarily set deadlines. Tell your employees that, if you can't trust them to meet deadlines, you can't trust them to do their job, and that is a huge problem . . . for them.

They tell you they can't do something you have delegated

This is fine, if – and only if – once you tell them how to do it or arrange for them to be told, the task gets done. If the answer is that it often doesn't get done, then the employee needs to go. They are not performing their job.

They question your direction

Because we often still have to prove to both sexes that we can do the job as well as men, it is almost acceptable to question our decisions. Unfortunately, it only takes one disrespecting sceptic on your team to undermine your authority. No one reporting to you should ever question your direction, and, if they do so, you need to jump all over it.

They take long lunches, call in sick, and/ or leave early

We have had our share of this in our office, not wanting to be big bitches and take our employees to task for bad behaviour. The problem with letting it go is that it will then happen again and again. By pushing the boundaries that you have set for them, they are testing you to see how much they can get away with. So act on it when you see it and don't let anything go.

They spend time on personal phone calls

We don't want to say that employees are like children, but sometimes you do feel like Mother when you are standing over them, tapping on your watch while they yammer on about their plans for the coming weekend. The point is that they will do as much as they can get away with; so you can't let them get away with anything. Your company is paying for their time, and, if they are spending it on a personal call, then they are stealing from the company.

They don't respond well when you point out an error

We had a senior publicist who would cringe when we pointed out errors, but never took responsibility for them, and an assistant who would give us ten reasons why it had happened. Neither of these responses is great. What you want to train your people to do is to acknowledge the mistake and take steps, either with you or on their own, to ensure that it won't happen again.

People do a careless and/ or casual job on most projects

If this is happening, you are being taken advantage of, especially if you swoop in at the eleventh hour to fine-tune the job before it goes out or is sent upstairs. Unfortunately, this is another trap that women managers seem to fall into more often than their male counterparts. Rather than confront someone with the fact that they did an unacceptable job, women will often want to fix it for them. Do this often enough and your employees will begin counting on the fact that you are not only going to cover their back but also do their job. The answer is simple: never accept mediocre work from your people.

There are pockets of employees who socialize throughout the day

A little bit of team bonding is a good thing, but too much of it is a waste of company money and can affect the profitability of your group. So break up the huddled masses at the water cooler by calling the ring leader into your office for a quick chat about the latest assignment. If you ignore it (again, women often want to be the good gal), then you are telling your staff that you don't care if they work.

Your employees don't stop talking when you enter a meeting

This is a really subtle demonstration of disrespect. When you, the manager of the team, the boss, the head honchette walk into a room, you should be met with quiet anticipation. If, however, you walk into a meeting and the group doesn't wrap up their conversation about the latest episode of *EastEnders*, you have a problem. They are showing you that they don't care that much about what you have to say. To take control back from the team, you need to start posturing a little. If you have an assistant, ask her to send an e-mail announcement that you have called a meeting. Make sure that it is outside your weekly meeting so it arrives unexpectedly. Create an agenda and send it round the day before so that the team knows you have set items to discuss. When you walk into the room, stand at the head of the table and make a statement that makes it clear that you are higher up the ladder and therefore privy to more information about the company than anyone else in the room. Something like 'I was at a meeting with the VPs this morning and there are a lot of changes in the pipeline', or 'It has been called to my attention that our team is a little behind on sales this month, and this has to turn around, starting today'. It doesn't have to be a negative statement, but there should be some stakes attached. If they think that you have information that will affect them personally, then you will have their undivided attention.

They're passing task back to you and *adding* to your to-do list, rather than making it shorter

Again, women seem to be suckers for employees-in-need. It takes a will of steel to deny the sweet project manager asking that something get taken off her plate or the young and eager columnist that needs you to rewrite her copy because you do it so much faster than she does. They work for you, which means you delegate down. If somehow you find that the work is flowing the other way, then it is time for you to start saying the dreaded 'n' word.

Gender Bending: Managing Men v. Managing Women

Male managers are not the only gender responsible for holding women back in the workplace. A female boss told us that she prefers to manage men because women need too much 'hand-holding'. Another woman preferred male employees because she felt that they weren't judging her. Yet another felt more comfortable delegating to men because with women she felt that she had 'to ask their permission'.

On the flipside, one manager we interviewed preferred women, because 'I feel it is my mission to encourage women to grow professionally and I feel more invested when I am helping an employee'. Anat Baron, an entrepreneur, had some sage advice for us: 'In my multiple careers I've always managed both men and women. I treated them the same. I'm a big believer in equality. Everyone gets a fair shake if they perform. I found in general that the stereotypes are true. Men are leery of a female boss (especially in male-dominated industries like hotels and beer) and are constantly testing you to see if you have what it takes. Women, on the other hand, are looking to be friends and are more open with their personal problems. They also expect you to be more understanding. My approach was to deal with everyone fairly. I was clear about expectations, gave people just enough rope, and constantly challenged them to exceed their own expectations of themselves. From the very beginning of my career I was keen to "develop" employees and was always thrilled to see them move up in their careers. I've always had a zero-tolerance policy for abuse of power, theft, greed, and outright lies. I was always considered a tough boss because I always spoke my mind, but I think most would consider me fair.'

Because of how we are socialized, it has become our instinct to treat men and women differently. Be aware of this inadvertently sexist behaviour – listening to men over women, asking women to get coffee, assigning the more high-profile assignments to men – and turn things upside down. Even better, be proactive about turning this dynamic around in the workplace and make an effort to mentor the women on your team. Encourage them to speak up and contribute in meetings. Divide both the glamorous and the dull assignments equitably between men and women. Alternate who makes copies, orders lunch, and cleans up after meetings. As a leader you have an amazing opportunity to do things better than the generation, or even just the boss, who preceded you.

The Boss's Boss: Protecting Your Staff from the Wrath Upstairs

Your boss wants you to make her life easier. She wants you to communicate the company's goals to the team and then work with the team to achieve them. Your boss is relying on you to share the appropriate amount of information with your staff. When you are new to the job, she will monitor your recommendations for promotions and punishment. Once you establish trust with your boss and are an effective spokesperson for your team, then those from below are expecting you also to be an effective spokesperson for the company and to share with them the goals and vision. They will want you to be their advocate too, to win the prestigious assignments, and to share their accomplishments with your boss. And when things get rough, when deadlines are missed, clients lost, or business slows, they want you to be their protector. So assure them that their jobs are safe and that you will take responsibility for whatever is going on with the higher-ups, and most of all let them know that you appreciate them and their contribution.

Girl Talk: Deborah Blackwell

Senior vice president and general manager of SOAPnet, Deborah Blackwell is responsible for all day-to-day operations of this quickly growing 24-hour soap opera channel. A well-respected and well-liked lady who leads, Deborah shared with us what she has learned while honing her skills – as a student at Harvard Business School, as an agent with William Morris and, in her current position at SOAPnet, as an effective leader.

How would you describe your job as a manager?
I view my job as defining and articulating a vision for
SOAPnet, getting the right people into the right jobs, and
then empowering and rewarding them.

Define your management style
'What do you recommend?' is a key phrase for me. When
people come into my office with a question I give them
the opportunity to solve the problem themselves. I have
found that people will rise to the challenge when I offer
them the opportunity. When people come in with
suggestions, my goal is that most of the time I take
employees' recommendations. That empowers your people
to take ownership of their role in the group.

*How do you inspire your employees to work harder and work
better?*
I am interested in people and I try to listen to them. I am
a big believer in praising in public and criticizing in
private. I make an effort to treat everyone in my team
with respect. I say to the team 'We will make mistakes.
Let's try things and see what happens.' I had an old boss
who said to me 'I am fine if you make mistakes, because,
if you are afraid to make them, then you won't try
anything.' And I see the value in that.

*What are your challenges when it comes to management and
how do you overcome them?*
Early on, I had difficulty giving clear direction. Because I
hated being bossed around, I would couch things as a
suggestion or an idea ('If you have time you might want
to so and so'), and finally an assistant said to me, 'I don't

know what you want me to do.' I was overcompensating for my discomfort with my role as an authority in the workplace. I realized that to get the best from people you need to delegate a clear assignment and set a deadline. I also learned that not everyone is ready for total empowerment. Some need more direction and for you to prepare an outline of the steps for a task.

Do you have any advice for first-time managers?
Accept that a work relationship is a different relationship, because, for it to run smoothly, there needs to be proper professional distance and that isn't always comfortable in the beginning. When I was promoted early on, I didn't understand why the secretaries treated me differently, were a bit colder, and no longer as chummy.

Do you enjoy working for and with women?
I adore working with women, and I have had two female mentors in my career who each taught me to 'own' my career and accomplishments. Every time I got a rise and promotion, the first would brush aside my gratitude and say, 'I am not doing this because I am nice; I am doing this because you are good.' The second trusted me to run a business – no small thing. I have worked with and for so many brilliant women that I feel like it is my responsibility to help women come along.

4

Don't Try This at Work: Ten Ways to Alienate Your Staff

Probably every single one of your friends has a story about the bitch boss from hell. The one who told us we were untalented and would never amount to anything; the one who disappeared for three-hour lunches, but carpeted us if we left five minutes early; the one who took credit for our ideas and blamed us for her mistakes.

This unfortunate management style has existed ever since Joan of Arc donned her final suit of armour and led her troops into a losing battle. The most common management mistakes are often surprisingly easy to identify and even easier to prevent. By taking a few simple precautions, we can all steer clear of these pitfalls and get the job done. In other words, you don't need to be a bitch to wield authority and command respect. Just the opposite, in fact.

Bad Boss Behaviour

1. You let your insecurities run the office

You have recently been promoted to manage a group of people who were, until this happy news, your professional peers. Looking over your newly acquired staff you sense resentment, hostility, and scepticism, rather than the warm friendly smiles you hoped for. You begin to doubt yourself. What do you have that they don't have? Sheila over there is better at public speaking than you are; how can you possibly tell her what to do? Mark had more sales last quarter than anyone on the team; why would he listen to you?

After your promotion you begin barking orders to overcompensate for the anxiety in the pit of your stomach. You begin to hide in your office. You leave for phantom very important lunches to avoid questions from your staff.

Stop! You are letting your insecurities run you, and the office.

The tiniest flicker of self-doubt can quickly balloon into a full-blown crisis of confidence. Helen Stephens, travel marketing coordinator for Bacardi, USA, suggests: 'When you start finding fault with everything and everyone, look into yourself. More likely than not, you are projecting your insecurities and fears.'

If you find yourself doubting your aptitude for your new position, ask yourself if the anxiety actually stems from your lack of professional skills or from a floundering self-esteem. If it is the latter, then the best advice (and we know it's easier to give than to follow) is to fake it until you make it. To do this you project more confidence than you really have. Stand up straight, breathe deeply, answer and ask questions directly, don't be afraid to say you don't know something, and don't agonize over decisions you have made. Again, posturing comes into play when you want to appear more comfortable in your management role than is really the case. To fake it with your boss, don't let self-doubt creep into your tone when you are presenting ideas, sales figures or campaign ideas. Your comfort level will increase the longer you are in your position and as soon as you sail through a tricky project.

If you determine that you do, in fact, lack certain skills, then tackle the deficiencies head-on: take a class, read a manual, and/or get some training (there are weekend seminars on almost everything these days, from management to marketing), so that you will no longer feel like a dope when you are talking to your staff about their areas of expertise. Keep this to yourself, however; the last thing you want is for your staff to make your remedial training the subject of water-cooler gossip. One woman we interviewed wrote to us to say, if you are insecure, 'Keep it to yourself! You are a leader but that doesn't come with the title. You have to earn the respect of your staff and if you behave like a child they will not respect you.'

Your insecurity can also impair the growth of your team. You might begin to alienate your staff through unintentional hostility, or to avoid tough assignments because you don't feel capable of leading your people through them. When we asked Liza, a former editor of a women's magazine, about this bad boss behaviour, she laughed and told us, 'OK. I did this. Totally. With the woman who had been hired the same week as me. It was extraordinary how she managed to massage every insecurity of mine, especially considering how underwhelmed I was by her skills and performance. I was always looking for her approval – I don't know why. Even worse, because we were in this weird position where technically she reported to me, but we were hired the same week and never got a chance to establish the pecking order, I tried to be her friend to overcompensate for my discomfort. I mean, I probably would've tried to be her friend anyway, but the situation was, like, the perfect storm that brought my managerial foibles to the surface.'

2. **You don't lead by example**

This is the situation where the standards you have for yourself are radically different from those you set for your employees. Admitting this behaviour takes brutal self-honesty. Do you often leave early, but expect your staff to stay late? Do you take long lunches, make personal calls, and spend a chunk of the Monday morning meeting talking about your weekend, but reprimand your employees if they do the same? We had a boss who unloaded all of her work on her underlings, took off every summer Friday, regardless of how busy it was, and worst of all, 'asked' her assistants to baby-sit her kids during their personal time.

None of that is cool. Being the boss doesn't mean that you're now entitled to lead a cushy life. On the contrary, you should be the hardest worker in the office. If, for example, your staff see that you are the first to arrive and last to leave, and that you rarely go out for lunch, then it's tough for them to find excuses not to work hard themselves. To gain the respect of those that work for you, it's essential that you lead by example, inspiring your staff to mimic your very own professional behaviour. Act as you would like your best employee to act. Jump in to help, don't talk about others behind their backs, be honest, work hard, respect others, and, most of all, enjoy the job.

Remember that you are the epicentre of the team and your behaviour, attitude, style, manner, sense of self, and ambition influence everyone around you. So, elevate the expectations you have for yourself and, with your capable and enthusiastic attitude, inspire those that report to you.

Good Witch or Big Bitch?

The boss 'friend'

Here's a story from our friend Mindy Pine.

With one boss, I fell into the trap – I thought we were friends. For three years, I loved working for her – and talking about *Sex and the City* on Monday mornings, and about shoes and make-up and shopping and all that kind of chat you do with a girlfriend over brunch. I worked for her when I met my husband, and she loved hearing all about our courtship. When we became engaged, my boss was one of the first people I wanted to call.

Cut to major changes at work, new structures, and suddenly I'm dropped. I'm out of the loop. Yes, I still have my job, but no chat time, no girlfriend time. She's too busy making friends with the new people who have joined our division. At a sales conference, she grabbed a few quiet minutes with me to catch up. She asked how my husband was doing, how was his job (I had shared many times with her how stressful it was). I said he was holding on.

A month later, I was told that my position was being eliminated and that there wasn't a place for me in the new organization. I then knew why she had been asking about my husband's job. This was almost the most upsetting thing to me. I had looked to her as a role model, someone who made a big salary in a male-dominated industry, an example of a woman making it in this business. Now my role model was making sure that my husband could take (financial) care of me. Worse than that, because of her interest in my personal life, I had thought we were friends.

Big Bitch. When asked what was the biggest mistake that they made as first-time managers, almost all of the women we interviewed said it was that they had befriended their employees. You are not there to be anyone's friend. You are in the leadership role to provide the tools and environment that your team needs to accomplish its goals. And, when you have blurred the lines of what should be a strictly professional relationship and then pull out the rug from under your employee when things get tough, you are a Big Bitch.

3. **You forget to take care of your own**

According to many women we interviewed, it is common for male bosses to be more comfortable around those of their own gender. Helen Stephens wrote to us to say: 'This familiarity is an instant "bond" with the known gender and, unless the manager makes a concerted effort to not play favourites based on sex, this behaviour is palpable and lethal in promoting the team atmosphere so needed in a department/office environment.' By the same token there are many female bosses who, because they have been socially conditioned to defer to men, will favour their male employees. So women in the workplace can often feel neglected by their male managers and overlooked by their female managers. Now that you are the chick-in-charge, it is your opportunity to run things differently. Be aware that you may be judging your female employees unfairly, based on male professional behaviour. Teach your female

employees to speak up for themselves. Give them
opportunities to shine by soliciting their input and ideas in
public meetings.

4. **You micromanage**

   If you are jumping in on every little decision, project phase
   and trip to the bank, then you are wasting both your time
   and your employees' time. One woman we spoke to said
   she began to 'just go through the motions' when she
   realized her boss wouldn't let her do anything on her own.
   If you are micromanaging then you are not maximizing
   their potential. When you treat your staff like children,
   guess what happens? They start acting like children,
   unable to make decisions without your input, and
   clamouring for your attention on projects big and small.
   But the main reason to avoid it? It means you are setting a
   poor managerial style, causing your staff to devolve rather
   than evolve and essentially shooting yourself in the foot.
   Many of the women we spoke to were guilty of
   micromanaging. Samantha Reese offers this insight. 'Sure
   I try not to micromanage, but I have been juggling two
   kids, a husband, ten employees, a dog, two houses, and a
   car for the past 15 years. To keep all the balls in the air I
   have to be pretty on top of everything, and it isn't so easy
   to let go.'

   Juli Tolleson, a director at US Concepts-Diageo Wine &
   Spirits, shares this story about the effects of micromanaging
   on your staff. 'I had an assistant account executive who was
   sometimes very slow to turn around important assignments.
   This made me panic at times, and I began to send her
   several e-mails requesting updates every time she had a
   project. This didn't go over well with her, and she began to
   either ignore my e-mails or give snappy responses. I was
   upset by the fact that she didn't seem to respect me very

much, but realized that she was generally nice and talented, and that I should talk with her to find out what I was doing wrong and figure out a way to make it work. She appreciated my going to her, explained that she felt like I was micromanaging her and that it interfered with her work, and made her less motivated to do the projects. I explained that I understood why that would be upsetting, but that she'd missed a few deadlines, so I felt nervous each time I gave her a time-sensitive project. I asked her what she suggested we do to fulfil both of our needs. She suggested a daily update e-mail, which was great. Moving forward, I stopped bugging her with update requests, and she made her deadlines. It worked because instead of me telling her what to do, I gave her the objective and asked her for the best solution. That made her feel empowered and respected, and eager to do good work. And I got what I needed, too.'

5. You're too controlling

There is a fine line between doing your job of managing and micromanaging. Micromanaging is formally defined as 'paying extreme attention to the small details'. In our daily work life it means having a manager over your shoulder at all times questioning your decisions, directing you on every aspect of an assignment, giving you zero autonomy, and not letting you make your mark. To make sure you are not one of these annoying and ineffective managers, answer this quick questionnaire.

1. Do you edit *everything* (even incidental correspondence to non-essential third parties)?
2. Do you check up on people several times a day while they are busy working on something you have assigned?
3. Do you insist on attending *every* meeting?

4. Do you find yourself questioning your employees' decisions (both big and small)?
5. Do you step in when your subordinates are trying to delegate to their staff?
6. Do you delegate only the inconsequential assignments?
7. Do you find yourself e-mailing your employees throughout the day with additional tasks, questions, instructions, requests for updates, etc. rather than consolidating these requests into global policies?

If you have answered 'yes' to more than a few of those questions, you are a control freak. Surprised? We didn't think so. To have reached this phase in your career, you have had to be on top of everything. And clearly you were good at it, because you have now been entrusted to manage others. But your job has changed and being a control freak about your own projects and career is very different from how you now need to guide others. You need to teach, explain, direct, and mentor your staff, not do their work for them. This is going to be a rocky transition as you begin to let go of the little stuff; so take it slowly. Reduce the number of times you check in with people by one, skip one or two meetings a week, let your staff delegate to their staff without input from you, and request a weekly status e-mail from your employees rather than daily.

Reasonable Expectations and Criticisms

As a junior sales executive (only a mini-step up from an assistant), Lisa Blake had an employer who expected her to come to the table with the sort of ideas, input, and solutions that come only with years of experience. For her, only a few months into a profession, this seemed insane. The employer's unreasonable expectations led to unreasonable criticisms as she was constantly berated and put down for not having more to offer. Eleven months into this job, she had to quit. Lisa ended up just fine; in fact, within four years, she had founded her own business. Just imagine how much her employer might have got from her over the years. As for reasonable criticisms, Trae Bodge, co-founder and creative director of Three Custom Color Specialists, says not to be afraid of criticizing or expecting things from your staff, pointing out, 'It's hard, especially when you work closely with someone, to comment on their work and how it could improve. But remember, you are doing something good for them as well as for the workplace, so it should (when done fairly) only strengthen your relationship.'

When assigning tasks, be realistic about the time frame you are setting for completion. It will help everyone if, as the manager, you are keeping track of what is on your employees' plates. Your people-pleasing staff members won't tell you when they are doing too much and will just take on more until they are buried. As manager, you need to be aware of their to-do list at all times. We had a situation with an employee who just kept taking on additional client work at team meetings. She would pipe up, hand held high, and say 'I would love to work on that' whenever we introduced a new project. When she began missing deadlines and the quality of her work started going downhill fast, we were really frustrated. We felt that she wasn't meeting our expectations – until we took stock of her to-do list and realized we were being completely unrealistic.

When setting your expectations for your employees, you also need to keep in mind their strengths and weaknesses. If you have an employee who is a great writer but not very fast, then don't assign them a project that has a short deadline. If you have someone who is a creative thinker but new to the business, understand that they won't be coming up with the winning ideas at a brainstorm but will help to move the thinking forward.

And lastly, be clear with the staff about what you consider to be a good job when you are assigning projects. The lazy boss is the one that delegates a task with little direction and no definition of success, and then explodes when their expectations are not met. If you want to see 30 units sold by next Thursday then tell your staff that is what you mean when you say 'Increase sales this week.' If you want a completed proposal by Sunday, say that rather than 'Get it done quickly.' If you define the expectations for your team and they are not met, then – and only then – you can reasonably criticize.

The Word: Dr Dorri Jacobs, Mediator

Dr Dorri Jacobs, a New York City work issues coach, mediator and internationally published author, gives us some advice about conflict resolution and firing, and suggestions for handling some of the stickier management situations.

Do you have thoughts for how we can become better managers?
Trust employee competence. Rather than criticize, allow individuals to explain where they could do better and what resources they lack (information, staff, equipment, time). Give praise often.

As a manager you are often put in the position of mediating. What is the goal behind mediating in the workplace?
Mediation empowers people to resolve their problems by working together. The parties involved have an opportunity to speak, to listen to each other, and to create and discuss possible solutions that will satisfy both of them.

Tips for firing someone with dignity?
Be honest. Be humane. Be kind. Give the person some notice, rather than expect him or her to leave the same day. If it is your decision, explain why she/he is being let go. If it is part of a major downsizing, and not your decision, say so. If it is a performance issue, make sure the employee knew about the problem and had been given an opportunity to improve. Give the employee a good reference letter and say potential employers can contact you as well.

Tips for conflict resolution?
Make sure there is enough time for all involved to express their needs and feelings and to really hear each other. No quick fixes: do not jump at the first 'solution' without verifying the reactions of each. Be willing to go further, if need be, so that they can come up with an answer that truly pleases each of them. Get training so that you are comfortable with conflict and with people talking on an emotional level.

6. **You treat your personal assistant like your husband, nanny, housekeeper, or best friend**
   To avoid treating your PA as anything other than an assistant, create a job description (containing only work-related tasks) before you interview candidates, and then stick to it when you have filled the post. Sounds easy, right? Not so, especially on those days when you are trapped in meetings all day and can't find 15 minutes to run to the bank, or when you are packing up for a sales conference and need to pick up your dry cleaning. If you don't want to be cast as an unprofessional boss from hell, please, please don't go off the list and ask your eager

assistant to get your shoes resoled, pick up nail polish for you, bank your pay cheque, buy a birthday card for your mother, or anything else that smacks of personal. Helen Stephens reminds us that your assistant 'will feel demeaned and eventually resentful of your assumption that she will also take care of you personally'. In most cases your assistant is being paid to assist you with your *job* only – so go ahead and ask her to book your travel for a business trip, but don't tell her to research your holiday in Morocco.

As for being a best friend, this is a distinctly female trap. Not enough of us have the right balance between being friendly but professional and being a friend. You can't be a friend to your employee, even though you may adore her. Your loyalty has to be to the company you work for, and you complicate things for both of you when you make a professional relationship personal.

A note about keeping things business-like in the office: don't go overboard. Believe it or not, it is possible to be *too* professional with your staff. We had a boss who didn't share a single bit of personal information with us. After two years of working for her we didn't know where she lived, if she was married, or even what she did before she arrived at the job. She didn't have so much as a personal photo on her desk or bookshelf. We knew that she was trying to maintain a proper distance, but it left her staff feeling unengaged. It was so extreme that when she left for a new job there was barely a murmur amongst the staff, and we quickly embraced her replacement. You want your team to support you, and even care about you enough to work hard for you. To make that happen they should like you, at least a little. We know it sounds counter-intuitive, but, by sharing a few key personal titbits with your staff, you become a living, breathing human being for them, not just an authority figure, and it is easier to work hard for a Jessica than a Boss. Do tell them where you went to college, how you found yourself in this career, about your first job experience, what you love about the profession, and even your favourite place to holiday. Don't tell them about the first time you got drunk, about your love life, conflicts that you may be having with others in the company, your long-term vision for your career, or any topic you cover in therapy. If you strike the perfect balance between too much information and not enough, your staff will both like you and respect you.

Seven Habits to Pass On

As a manager you have a captive audience. You can set the bar for how your people act and perform as members of your team. You also have the young and eagers looking to you for how to behave professionally, so teach them well. To get the best from everyone on a day-to-day basis, demonstrate great work habits.

Be clean
Don't have paperwork stacked on your desk, artwork askew, extra shoes piled in the corner, half-full coffee mugs, and dying plants in your office. If you maintain a clean, professional office space, the chances are they will, too.

Handle Q&As well
When your team approaches you with a question, answer it straightaway. If you don't know the answer, then say so but that you will find out. It will teach your employees not make up answers because they are too ashamed to admit they don't know something. Similarly, you can inspire your team to tackle problems the right way by demonstrating

that, when you are faced with one, you find out all of the details before offering an off-the-cuff solution.

Keep on top of to dos

Teach your team to spend a few minutes at the end of each day to jot down the to-do list for the next day. It is an efficient way to use those last 20 vacant minutes of the day.

Remember e-mail is not snail mail

When your team sends you e-mails, answer them right away. You don't want to make them wait for answers they need to proceed with their work, and you also don't want to imply that it's okay to procrastinate.

Be on time

Turn up for everything *on time*. If you are late to meetings, appointments, reviews, or anything else, you are demonstrating that you are fine with poor timekeeping. Since you are teaching them to be ideal employees, teach them to be on time.

Look professional

Again, even if you believe that you get more creative thinking done in your favourite pair of jeans, don't wear them to the office. You want to inspire your employees to dress professionally.

Always be prepared

When presenting to your team or your client, make sure you are prepared. Not only does it help you with your own level of confidence, but it encourages your staff to hone their own knowledge before jumping into a meeting or presentation.

7. **You think your employees are telepathic**

    Do you want your employees scurrying around you anxiously because they are trying to work out exactly what it is that you want them to do and how you want them to do it? We hope the answer is 'Of course not!'. That's what happens when you expect people to be telepathic. While someone who has worked with you for a while might have developed instincts regarding your preferences, that's almost never the case with new people. Make it easier on everyone by reviewing directions and expectations clearly and concisely. Remember that too many people fill in a lack of information with negative assumptions (she doesn't like me–she is avoiding me–I am going to be fired–I did something wrong); so give your employees a break and tell them exactly what you want.

8. **You take credit without giving it**

    It is pretty bad to take credit for other people's work and worse when you never give nods for jobs well done. Before you skip this paragraph because you think that it couldn't possibly apply to you, consider this scenario: your boss has assigned you a report to write and you pull in your team to help you with the project. Two weeks after handing it in, the boss has finally had a chance to review it and calls you into the office to say 'well done!' The rest of the day gets hectic, and you don't mention the feedback to the team. Are you taking credit without giving it? Yes. Is it intentional? Maybe not. Would your boss have wanted you to praise your team at that moment? Maybe, maybe not. Perhaps she assumes that having a crackerjack group is part of your job. Either way, moments after leaving the boss's office, a good manager pulls together everyone that contributed to the report to congratulate and praise them, or at least sends the team an e-mail. They made you look good, and for that they deserve credit and thanks. If one too many instances goes by where you don't take the time to acknowledge their contribution, you will be stuck with a staff that lacks ambition, interest, and engagement.

9. **You cry, shout, or lose your temper**

Almost everyone we interviewed for this book had a bad boss story that featured a woman who was a shouter or crier. This is unfortunate, because we get a bad rap in the workplace for being over-emotional anyway, and it only takes a few criers out there in the corporate world to perpetuate the stereotype. If you scream only occasionally and cry only once in a blue moon, that is still far, far too often. If you have got to the point of exhibiting any extreme emotion in the office, you have failed somewhere along the line and need to rein your emotions back in. If you are a shouter, then try the ten second method. When something angers you, before responding or tackling the issue, take a breath that lasts five seconds going in and five seconds going out. By the time you are taking the second breath, you should be calm enough to discuss something without yelling. If you are a crier, there are many reasons to turn this behaviour around. First and foremost, people lose respect for bosses who cry. Imagine you are in your boss's office; she has just received the news that the company has lost an account and has started crying in front of you. Beyond awkward, this behaviour is downright strange. As adults, crying is just not the thing to do. It doesn't inspire confidence or respect. It does inspire compassion, sympathy, and maybe a little pity. But do you want to be pitied by your assistant? The worst aspect of this behaviour is that you are giving off the vibe that it is okay to be highly emotional in the workplace, when it isn't.

10. You're a jealous Julie

Jealousy is an insidious emotion that rears its ugly head in the most inappropriate ways. Sometimes you are faced with managing someone who is a brilliant and creative thinker or even someone who has more potential than you do (only if you are really honest with yourself would you ever admit this). If you don't know yourself very well and find yourself treating this blessed employee worse than everyone else, jealousy could be at work. We spoke to entrepreneur Anat Baron, who had a 'jealous Julie' in her life. 'When I had a producing deal, I worked with (not for) a head of development who was in my hair all the time. She had to know who I was talking to, eating lunch with, etc. When it came time to renew my deal, I was in Europe attending a friend's wedding. She was so petty and jealous that she didn't get invited (the couple were another producer and an agent) that she ensured that my cheques stopped coming, and that I found out about it while I was away. I came back and packed up my stuff. Life is too short to be around that type of energy.' If you feel resentment towards an employee, keep in mind that it is just your competitive nature gone awry and remind yourself that if your employee succeeds then you succeed.

Girl Talk: Louise Jordan

To understand the other point of view, we spoke to Louise Jordan, an account executive at Deussen Global Communications about her thoughts on being managed.

Did you notice any management characteristics that were common among your female bosses?
They can be too emotional. Often, I have had female bosses who, if they are having a bad day, somehow think that makes it okay to take it out on me. Also, in many cases, I think I was threatening to them. Instead of wanting to take more of a mentor role and be happy to help me grow, it was almost like they wanted to hold me back. In the worst cases, it was straight out jealousy.

Did many of your female bosses try and befriend you rather than keep it professional?
Yes, I had this one boss who always wanted me to go out with her etc., which was fine, but then, when I couldn't go or I had something else to do, it was very uncomfortable because I felt like I was hurting her feelings, and she would act a little pissed off at me during the work day. It was like being stuck between a rock and a hard place.

That being said, I do think that you can have a friendship with your boss; it doesn't have to be all business all the time. I mean, we are all human.

But there just has to be an understanding that there is a boss-employee boundary that you can't cross, and as the boss you can't abuse your power over your employee.

How do you like to be managed?
I like a boss to give me a project or a task, explain in detail what they want (but allow flexibility if I have ideas or thoughts), and then let me run with it. Then we meet back to discuss how it is going and any changes that need to be made, etc. This way I feel like we are connected, but I am not being micromanaged.

Also, it is really important to give positive feedback. All people want to feel like they are doing a good job. Of course, they have to be doing a good job to get positive feedback. I had a boss who never told me I was doing anything right. It was always what I was doing wrong, and that really frustrated me no end and made me not want to do well. It is really discouraging if you feel like nothing you do is good enough.

What did you learn from previous managers?
Having had challenging managers, I actually think I am going to be a good one. I think I am much more patient than I used to be because I had one boss who was so moody and hard to work with that I learned to just relax, be calm, and let her bad mood blow over. In the past, I would have got really upset and let it get to me. Now I have learned that getting emotional in the work place is never a good idea. It is better to walk away and calm down. That being said, I also learned to speak up for myself. I mean just because you have to work for someone, doesn't mean they can treat you any way they want.

Anything else you want to share?
One last point, in a business world where men still make more than women do for the same jobs, and 95% of all CEO and top positions are held by men, I think that women should support and help each other, instead of feeling threatened by another woman. I know this has been said time and time again, for many things, but it is true. In a way, it has been very good for me to be so poorly managed by a couple of women bosses, because I know that I will never do that when I'm the boss.

5

Communicate, Motivate, Celebrate

*N*ow that you have a solid team in place, how do you keep it motivated and happy? In all the books we've read, in all the interviews we've done, and in all the research we've seen, the advice is the same: communicate. Communicate in a positive way. Share good news. Criticize privately, praise publicly. Have an open-door policy. Don't talk, listen. There really is no *I* in team. Create *we*. It all sounds great, but how do you actually do it?

A human resources director of a 400-person engineering firm with offices in New York, New Jersey, Pennsylvania, and Florida told us that, in her exit interviews with more than 50 employees in the last six months, they all gave the same reason for leaving: 'Not enough communication from senior management.'

Not enough communication from management? If you had asked us a couple of years ago for the main reason why people leave jobs, we would have undoubtedly said because they want to make more money. But what we're hearing over and over is that communication is key. Employees want to know what's expected of them. Libby Sartain of Yahoo! says that in her 30-year career she's noticed that most people come to work every day wanting to give their best and add value. And if they do what's expected of them, they want to know they can expect in return.

Naturally, part of the return is compensation. But there is so much more. Remember, people *want* to do a good job. So how do you help them do a good job – and keep them motivated and inspired when they come to work each day? How do you give your team what they need to succeed? This chapter looks at what good managers can do to keep their employees happy.

It's a Two-way Street

Goodness, there are a lot of unhappy people in the workplace! Searching around the Internet we found a number of sites where people complain about their bosses, including www.iworkwith fools.com, www.oddtodd.com, and www.revengelady.com, as well as sections on www.ivillage.co.uk where people can anonymously post complaints about their bosses and co-workers. There's even a blog-hosting community at www.fthisjob.com that says: 'Welcome to fthisjob.com, the "I hate my job" blogging community. Here at fthisjob.com, we believe that job blogging helps you better deal with those ass customers, stupid boss decisions, and other daily crap you get at work . . .'

'Other daily crap you get at work'? That's a terrible attitude. Yes, we've all had crappy jobs, but can you honestly say that all of the time it was because your managers were useless? Can't you admit, once in a while, that your skills didn't match up to the position? We can.

Early in our careers, both of us worked at the same high-energy public relations company. It was our first experience at an actual agency, and, boy, was it eye-opening. We were impressed by the people we worked with — they were smart, highly motivated, and results-oriented. From the minute you entered the door, you knew you had to perform or move on. There was no real training, yet everybody seemed to excel. It was exciting and scary at the same time. Each day we felt we were one mistake away from losing our jobs. We learned as much as we could, did as well as we could, and got the hell out of there in a year. Somehow, though, that agency made a lasting impression on us. We now greatly admire the principal of the agency and even seek out his advice for our business. We don't want to run our shop in the same manner, yet we marvel at the calibre of people whom he consistently hired and the quality of work he was able to get out of them. It wasn't always pleasant, but it was certainly productive. And, if we were to be really honest, we would admit that we didn't do our best work there and it wasn't management's fault. Yet when you read these complaint-filled websites, you never see anyone take responsibility for their part. They are all victims of bad management and bad communication.

When faced with bad management, we offer the same advice that your therapist will give you when you're in a bad relationship. Examine yourself. Look honestly at your performance and your own communication skills and see if you can make any changes to your approach so you will get a better result. Remember, there are two sides to every story.

The Word: Judith Glaser, Author

Judith is author of Creating We: Change I-Thinking to WE-Thinking and Build a Healthy, Thriving Organization.
She calls herself an organizational anthropologist and coach. She brings new insights to leaders by creating 'we-centric' workplaces that support the growth and development of people, partnerships, and a thriving business. As a master coach, facilitator, and organizational designer, she works with clients to raise the bar and achieve the next level of success through a process she calls the *journey*. This process catalyses new ways of thinking and new types of courageous conversations, and enables leaders to redefine challenges, rethink strategies, reinvent products and services, build strong partnerships with clients, leverage mergers and acquisitions, and create new business models that drive profitability and growth, all with a direct line of sight to the customer.

Her clients span a wide variety of industries and are organizations looking to sustain a leadership position by revitalizing their strategic business focus in order to become more competitive, profitable, and higher performing. They include Siemens, Pfizer, Coach Inc., Lipton, VeriSign, Thomson, Novartis, Verizon, Citibank, Donna Karan International, Exide Technologies, and Clairol Inc. She shares her thoughts on creating a positive environment through healthy, we-centric conversations.

- You have to remember that there's a human being on the other end of a conversation. I encourage my clients to listen without judgment, and every time I remind them that the premier skill set for an effective leader is to create space for other people, not take it away. You should know that words will either cause us to bond and trust more fully and think of others as friends and colleagues, or they will cause us to break rapport and think of others as enemies.

- Through my years of consulting, I've noticed that as you grow up into a business, you're driven from position of power to position of power, from one box to another. If you're driven only by positional power then you start to assume the kinds of behaviour that destroy companies. In my book I list the main behaviour patterns that cause companies and executives to fail:
- Lack of shared focus, shared purpose, and/or shared vision.
- Lack of enterprise-wide communication.
- Lack of organizational ambition and a strategic approach for getting there.
- Lack of respect for others in the organization.
- Failure to tap resources and inner talent, creativity, and responsibility.
- Failure to break down walls ('silos') between divisions.
- Lack of team cohesion and failure to develop team agreements, rules of engagement, and decision-making processes.
- Failure to focus outside and see the customer.
- Lack of hope and spirit; a punishing environment.

To allow for executives and companies to succeed, they must have the ability to:

- have healthy conversations that build a sense of common purpose, and assert a strong leadership voice and laser-sharp focus on the work that needs to be done

- clarify organizational ambition, and create a strategic focus that encourages employees to step out of their comfort zones and take action in the face of ambiguity
- leave behind the toxic, emotional baggage of the past and tap into new resources and under-used talents by encouraging creativity and responsibility
- exchange knowledge and wisdom between groups
- have vital conversations that challenge all parties in creative ways
- create and live by team agreements, rules of engagement, and a clear decision-making process
- redefine challenging circumstances in creative ways, to tell new stories with an external focus that connect the needs of customers, exploit and shape future trends, and reposition business for category leadership
- focus on the positives, celebrate success, grow from failure, and build hope and spirit into the organizational DNA, in order to repeatedly create and achieve critical milestones of success
- most importantly, find one's voice and be fearless in creating a 'we-centric' organization that fosters an attitude of 'We are in this together'

The 'M' Word: Learn to Love Good Meetings

We're not big fans of meetings. We're a small company in an open-plan office where communication just happens. We listen to each others' conversations, glean what we need to know, keep our heads down and get the work done – in our case, generating media results for our clients. Or so we thought. We found that our 'eavesdrop your way to success' method of communication wasn't happening. Goals weren't being met. Staff didn't know what was expected of them or what their priorities were. Where had we gone wrong? We were trying to create a culture where people acted as we did: they knew what they had to do and did it. How could we so quickly forget our early career experience?

We had to find a way to give the team what they needed. We were surprised when the answer presented itself in the place where we would have never considered looking – a meeting. We had a horrible staff meeting one morning when found out that the placements (articles written about our clients) we needed were not happening. We had to set the goals in very specific terms for one of our publicists. We told her exactly what we needed and when it was due. We both felt terrible. If that had happened to either of us in a meeting, we would have died of humiliation. Yet what we found was an amazing transformation. Without the weight of working out her goals and deadlines, our publicist was free to execute – and she did so brilliantly. She's an excellent publicist, just not a good time-manager. So we have to help her to structure her time. Not a big deal, if it helps her excel at her job. Remember, if she excels, we excel. See Chapter 6 for more advice on getting the most from meetings.

Focus On the Future: Career Development Planning

The hardest thing for a business to recover from is the loss of an employee. Even a mediocre one has been trained and can be coached to the next level. It's important to think as much about your individual employee's future within your organization as it to think about meeting your sales goal. Creating career development plans is a great way to get you and your employees on the same page about their future.

A career development plan lays out a list of long- and short-term goals for each employee, both for the job they are in and the one they are working towards. For example, a sales person will have not only their sales goals listed, they will also have benchmarks they are required to reach before they will be promoted to sales manager.

Also, outline a planned sequence of formal and informal experiences to assist employees in achieving their goals. It's important to discuss employees' personal hopes and dreams as well. Libby Sartain at Yahoo! had finished a career development plan with one of her employees just before we interviewed her. She explained that personal goals often figure prominently in the plans. This employee had young children at home and he wanted to make sure that he wouldn't be relocated or asked to travel for long periods at a time. He made it clear that his future in the company was linked to remaining in the San Francisco Bay area. If you are working on a plan with an employee, they should have a tremendous say in their future, because you want to retain the best people in your team.

Career development goals should be linked to the person's potential. The purpose of the plan is to help the employee to achieve these goals. Because the manager has helped the worker to consider how to achieve career goals within the organization, the likelihood of the organization also retaining the employee increases.

Another benefit of the career development plan is to help employees to set realistic expectations for their movement up the ranks. The plan should suggest time frames for certain milestones like promotions, and identify specific areas that need to develop before the next milestone. The plans aren't commitments, but rather a road map for the future and an explanation of your half of the bargain: 'If you do this, this, and this, then you should expect that, that, and that.'

Here are the steps for career development planning.

- Have a meeting with your employee to identify their career interests. Specifically, ask them to outline their goals for the short term (one year) and the long term (two to five years). Also ask them about their current job: are they interested in receiving special assignments, participating in training courses, acquiring new skills, or contributing in new ways to the department?
- Don't forget to ask about family and community goals. Are they able to relocate or interested in doing so?

- After the meeting, sit down with your management colleagues and work out if you can deliver on the employee's desired goals. If you can't, you need to try and find out why and to propose an alternative solution.
- Prepare the plan and arrange another meeting with the employee to review it. Give them a copy and put one in their personnel file. Make sure you track their progress throughout the year and discuss it during their performance review. If they are way ahead, adapt the plan accordingly. If they are way behind, try to get them back on track, or adapt the plan accordingly.

Good Witch or Big Bitch?

Some bitches are crazy
This is a scary story from our friend Aleta Jones.

On the last day of my honeymoon, I was hired as managing editor of a bridal website, which was then an umbrella site for several different magazines – an unhappy arrangement, to say the least. The site was about to go through a major upgrade of its operating system, which had been custom designed according to the specifications of my boss, Justine. In fact, the notion to make the bridal website the umbrella for too many magazines was Justine's, one I imagine she was able to execute because, as I would soon learn, she screamed so much and so hysterically, that people must have said 'Yes' just to get her out of their offices. The week I was hired, Justine had also hired an editorial assistant who would function as her assistant as well. This was the second week of November. On the Thursday of my first week, Justine announced she was resigning and wouldn't be back after Thanksgiving. Her promise was that in the two and a half weeks that remained, she'd make herself available to train us. I was told that I would take over the editing of the site, without a pay rise, her office, or her assistant.

The next two weeks were like a bad dream that just kept getting worse. A typical incident: I go to Justine's office with a question about some aspect of the functionality of the new system. The door is open; I knock and step in. Justine is on the ground on her hands and knees. I say, 'Justine?' She screams 'Not now! I'm doing something really important!' It turns out she was looking for a bead that fell off her necklace. Now, I respect the role of jewellery in one's life as much as anyone, but *really*. This was her idea of being available and about the extent of the knowledge transfer I got from her about the new system. I'm still amazed by the profound lack of responsibility for the website, the project, and her hires that she demonstrated in that period. What was even worse, though, than her behaviour towards the staff, was the extent to which she had alienated nearly every department she worked with, especially Information Technology. Not only was I thrust into a role that I was unprepared for, but I had to spend six months rebuilding bridges that she had burned to a crisp. The icing on the cake? She tried to recruit me for the start-up she was leaving for.

Sometimes, managers are just crazy. If you're lucky, they will resign or get sacked. If they don't leave, then find another job, or another manager.

We All Win! Goal-Setting to Bring Your Team Together

Individual goals. Team goals. Departmental goals. Corporate goals. At every level and every step of the way you need goals to succeed. Most of the self-help books on the market will tell you that the first step to achieving your goal is to say it out loud – and then write it down.

Individually, and as an organization, setting goals gives you long-term vision and short-term motivation. It focuses you on the acquisition of knowledge and helps you to identify and organize your resources so you can better achieve your goals.

Goal setting helps you to:

- decide what's important
- separate the relevant from the irrelevant
- motivate yourself to achieve your goals
- improve your performance
- improve your self-confidence by keeping track of your successes

A good goal statement needs to be specific. It needs to be measurable, action-oriented, realistic, and tangible. Big goals (*I want to write a book*) should be broken down into smaller goals (*Come up with an idea. Create an outline. Research. Write a proposal. Find an agent etc.*) and then written down. Make a commitment to accomplish each goal, and then remind yourself to stay on track by setting deadlines. Don't forget to review and re-assess your goals on a regular basis.

Goal-setting for organizations is as important as it is for individuals. Your team needs to know what they are trying to achieve and how they fit into the bigger picture. When we were in book publishing, we had a manager who used to say, 'Don't think like a publicist. Think like a publisher' – meaning don't focus on generating placements; focus on generating placements *and* putting out messages that will sell books. The goal wasn't to generate placements but to sell books.

Put Your Money Where Your Mouth Is: Pay and Sense

Second to good communication is good money. And we would argue, that even if an employee worked in a communication utopia, if another company with horrible communication offered to double their salary for the same position, they'd be out through the door in a heartbeat.

What's really fair? The Internet is a great place to find out: visit sites such as www.salaryexpert.com or www.payfinder.com. Depending on the type of business you own or run, you could also visit the Department of Trade and Industry's website for information on the minimum wage at: www.dti.gov.uk/er/nmw.

Ten Simple, Cost-effective Ways to Show Appreciation and Earn Good Will

1. Sending employees to external training sessions is a win-win. They feel valued, love the day out of their routine, and you get back an enthusiastic employee with a new skill to offer the organization. Sarilee Norton, president of the Tru-Tech Business for Temple Inland, noticed a highly motivated member of her administrative support team. There were a number of personnel changes in her department and the employee had stepped up to fill in. Sarilee wanted to do something to reward her extra efforts. The employee had expressed interest in Powerpoint; so Sarilee told her to find a one-day course in the area and sign herself up. She was thrilled, and when she returned she began creating presentations for the management team – making a further contribution to the company.

2. Put non-managers in charge of non-critical projects. Chrisi Colabella is the president of a construction leads service called CIS (Construction Information Systems). Her staff love to go on company outings – baseball games, picnics, Christmas parties. She hates planning them, but is happy to let her staff appoint someone to lead the party effort. She assigns a budget and leaves the rest to them. The staff love the responsibility of planning the events and contributing to the increased morale of the organization.

3. Acknowledge birthdays. We love birthdays, but the celebrations can quickly get expensive and disruptive. Pick a gesture, set a budget, and do the same for everyone when the occasion arises. If money is tight, a nice card signed by everyone in the department and a bouquet of flowers is a good gesture.

4. Try and think of rewards that are unexpected. Sarilee Norton may just be the cleverest rewarding manager we know. She's always trying to find ways to reward extra effort. She recommends you take a minute and really think about what will make people happy. She had a production manager who was performing above and beyond. Her company often gets tickets to stock car racing events for customers, who are escorted by her sales force. When an extra ticket became available she offered it to her production manager. Another win-win: he felt appreciated and the customers got the opportunity to meet the person who was actually producing their product.

5. Praise in front of the team. It's easy to do and makes people feel important.

6. We all love a little pampering. Think about gift tokens for a manicure or a massage, or tickets for a football match as a way for saying thank you for a job well done.

7. The team lunch: consider throwing a pizza party when a big goal is reached. It's inexpensive and great way for the team to bond and let off steam. If you have it on Friday, there's no reason why you can't splurge for a few beers, too. If you choose to have a beer, make sure it doesn't get you drunk.

8. Bring junior people to networking events, business social functions, or meetings. It's important for their career growth and it feels like a big perk. Just make sure you brief them properly on what the event is, what they should wear, and what is expected of them.

9. Late night etiquette. If people are expected to work late and they are not eligible for overtime, it is important to acknowledge their additional effort. Make sure they have safe and free transportation home. Buy them dinner if they're working late into the evening. Make sure no one is alone or feels unsafe. Have employees escorted through dark car parks. A good rule of thumb: if you wouldn't want your child or spouse put in the situation, you probably shouldn't put your employee in it either.

10. Inter and intra company recognition. If there is a communication tool in your organization, make sure your team's successes are championed. State specifically the goals achieved and name names.

Girl Talk: Shar McBee

Shar McBee is a motivational speaker and author of *To Lead Is to Serve*. She had not received any management training when suddenly she was put in charge of a staff of 500 people. A wise mentor taught her a secret – think about what you can give, not what you can get. She tried it. It worked amazingly. Since then Shar has taught the secret to thousands. In the 1980s Shar set out on a quest for deeper meaning. For ten years she travelled around the world working with relief organizations in a dozen countries. Today, Shar McBee is the president of SMB Publishing, Inc. Her mission is to transform new managers into joyous leaders. She is currently working on the second book in her Joy of Leadership series. With an empowered group of people on your side, nothing can stand in your way. Shar shares her 'secret' for motivating people with us.

Tell us about your philosophy and how you came to it.
I was put in charge of a very large special event. I was responsible for 500 people. I had a specific plan for how I wanted the event to be executed and I shared it with the team. I thought I had prepared them for everything. What I hadn't prepared for was the fact that the event was massively oversold. We had thousands of people show up and nowhere to put them. My army of ushers was crumbling. They weren't seating people as I had trained them. They weren't being polite to the guests. They were herding them like cattle. I was beside myself. I started criticizing and trying to get this beleaguered force back in

action. I was frustrated and angry. I went to my mentor, who had given me the assignment, and told her what I was dealing with and asked for advice. She asked me if I had given the ushers lunch. I was shocked. Of course I hadn't thought about it. All I could think about was what I needed, what I had prepared, my plan, and my plan in disarray. When I turned the situation around and started thinking about what they needed to get their job done, I was humbled. I started giving them support and encouragement and was amazed. Things turned around, and they began working together as we had prepared. I teach people to come at things from the 'give' side, not the 'get' side. My whole joy of leadership method is based on the feeling that if you want to be happy, you want to be giving.

It sounds great, but how do we actually get on the 'give' side? First stop thinking about how you can get someone to do what you want. Think always about what you can give for them to succeed. It's the most natural thing in the world. Look at nature. Nature is only giving and not getting. Take avocados: if you give an avocado seed to the earth, then it will give you a whole world of avocados.

I realize this is difficult. When you are under a lot of pressure or feel scared, you automatically contract. Here's another example. If you're stuck in a traffic jam, stop thinking, 'How can I get out of here?' Think, 'What can I give here?' Maybe all you have to give is your calmness. Maybe you can give people a break. Maybe you can give an inch and the traffic will actually open up.

Remind yourself that all people want is to do a good job.

Where do you begin?

The beauty of this is that you can begin immediately. It doesn't cost you time and it doesn't cost you money. It has to start with you. Most people want the other person to become giving. So first have a discussion with your team. Talk about your new philosophy and your own experience. Even people who are extremely sceptical eventually come around. The funny thing about giving is that it is energizing and not depleting. When you're being giving, you feel good. When you hold a discussion with a group of employees about this topic, the group is energized.

What is the benefit of giving?

Remember, the number one reason why people quit is not because of the work but because of hurt feelings. If you want to keep your workforce happy, then you're going to have to focus on what they need to be successful and give it to them.

The boss needs to be creative enough to take time to see if a project or task is right for an individual. Remember delegating is not dumping. It's about giving people projects that are matched with their talents, and then sitting back and watching them succeed.

You say that your philosophy also applies to time management. How?

When people go wrong in this area, it's because they start focusing on the work instead of the people. Never forget that your number one priority is your people. It's very easy to lose sight of that. The really successful managers know how to support their people so that they can do the work. A lot of managers make the mistake of thinking that the work is more important, but really it's the people.

I remember going into a restaurant once, a big chain, and they had a manager who was always totally stressed. He was constantly running around like a maniac, clearing tables, writing bills, directing staff. He was nervous, and his people showed the effects. Another time, I came when a different manager was on duty. She was sitting at a corner table in the restaurant, looking as relaxed as can be. I wondered how she did it, especially given the other manager's frenetic pace. I sat down and asked her about it. 'It's simple,' she replied, 'My job is supporting the team. I find out what they need and give it to them. I don't focus on the table that needs to be cleared. I focus on the people.' She had more time because her people were operating more successfully.

Delegation Is Not a Dirty Word: Employing Your Employees

For some bosses, one of the most uncomfortable aspects of bossdom is telling others what to do. The discomfort isn't entirely unwarranted; there *is* a delicate balance between assigning as much as possible to others and simply dumping your workload on those around you just because you can. But this is a balance every manager has to get to grips with. You've earned the title of Lady Who Leads, and now you have to take charge and delegate responsibly and with respect for yourself and your employees.

Most of the time, of course, you probably *could* do it better and faster yourself, but that doesn't allow your employees to grow, nor does it give you room to spread your wings and develop your own managerial and leadership skills. If you make a plan and assign tasks thoughtfully, everybody will win.

Get Over It: How Not to Be Afraid of Your Employees!

A staggering percentage of leaders are scared of their staff. Have you had a manager who was never available when you needed her? Who picked up her phone as soon as you knocked on her door? Missed team meetings or let other people lead them? Are you that type of manager?

Anxiety about facing the staff seems especially common among women, many of whom overcompensate and become the bitch bosses we have all encountered on the way up the ladder. It's not fair, but women bosses are judged more harshly than their male counterparts. We are socialized to accommodate, not confront, and when you are a manager, everything can feel like a confrontation. Women often feel self-conscious when assigning tasks, or uncomfortable when having to reprimand an employee. It is hard for many of us to find comfort in the 'it's just business' mantra chanted by male professionals.

The upshot is that we often take too much on ourselves so that we don't have to tell someone else to do it, accept mediocre work, are taken advantage of, or go overboard and mimic the male style of management, which is often dictatorial. This fear of confrontation can make it difficult to feel comfortable with your authority, get the best work from your employees, and efficiently manage the day-to-day delegation that is necessary to get your job done. So, any way you look at it, if you want to be a good manager (and keep your job), you have to get over fearing your employees.

Here are a few things to tell yourself before facing your staff.

- You were hired for a reason.
- Your skills are different from everyone else's, but obviously (since you got the job) a better fit for your position.

- Your boss has faith in you; so prove him or her right.
- You are not doing your employees a favour in the long run by accepting mediocre work from them.
- You have skills and experience that is worth sharing with your staff.
- The employees need to prove themselves to you, too.
- You love this profession and you want to share your enthusiasm with your team.

No Dumping: How to Delegate with Respect

Delegating is assigning tasks, projects, and responsibilities with thought and with the understanding that you are there to offer support along the way. *Dumping* is handing over to dos without explanation or guidance. Delegating without respect will quickly label you as a bitch. And unfortunately, as women, we have to work out how to hand over without pissing off. Don't assign anything that you wouldn't do or haven't done yourself. If possible, know how to do what you are delegating, even the simplest day-to-day tasks, such as how to use the copier or call for a messenger. 'When assigning jobs to my employees, I try to see to the strength of the individual. Then I will entrust a project or a portion of a project to an employee to manage. This gives them a stronger investment in the job and the organization,' says Susan Goldbetter, executive director of Circuit Productions, Inc.

Trying to put the task in a larger context for your staff is a learning opportunity. For instance, if you need to ask your assistant to stuff 1,000 envelopes for a client event, take two minutes to tell her about the goals of the event and how your team is the best group to achieve them. Treat every task with respect. Yes, boxing up and shipping out items is mundane and mind-numbing, but if you are unapologetic about assigning it – recognizing that it is crucial to your business – your employee won't feel embarrassed about doing it. Whenever possible, also explain how an assignment fits into her professional development. If you work in retail, say, and it's time for the pre-Christmas stock-take, put it to the staff as a way for the team to become knowledgeable about the merchandise before the rush. If you work in PR, tell your publicity assistant that labelling the 200 envelopes going to book reviewers is a way for her to get to know key media names. What we know and need to share is that *the road to learning is doing,* and that those new to the business need to start by *doing* the basics.

Once you've explained the context of a delegated task, make sure your people have the tools they need to get it done. Be clear with your directions; for example, if you are asking someone to present at a coming conference, make sure you provide her with all of the relevant details, including subject, length of presentation, and audio/visual needs. Be available to answer questions and help with problem solving. If appropriate, make other staff members available to help. Be specific about your expectations, including due dates and, most importantly, how you will define success.

Tamara Lawson, CFO for InnVest Real Estate Investment Trust, explains: 'The only time I wouldn't delegate is if something is very time-sensitive and important and it is faster to do it myself, or if I am the only one able to do something. I find the latter is rarely the case, since I am always looking for opportunities to give the people I manage the chance to develop new skills.'

Working Together: It's All About the Team

When delegating to a group, the assignment is usually more complicated than a few steps and will most likely involve several employees of varying levels of seniority. Your chances of a project going smoothly increase exponentially when you follow these steps.

- Set goal(s)/objective(s) for the team.
- Assign responsibilities and deadlines for senior team members.

- Meet senior team members individually to divide the responsibilities into steps.
- Set progress meetings for the team.
- Be available for questions and assistance.
- Proactively check with key employees to see how it's going; don't wait until the last second for a possible catastrophic surprise.

When assigning responsibilities, don't expect everyone to contribute to the same degree; treat them and value them as individuals. To avoid conflict and tension within the group, clearly define both reporting procedures and individual responsibilities. And no matter what your feeling about a given project is, always show your staff enthusiasm and energy. As the leader, the group is looking to you for an emotional cue. If you are enthusiastic about it, then they will be, too. If you convey resentment or anxiety, then don't be surprised if the project becomes contentious or is executed in below par fashion.

Be Kindly: Why Positive Reinforcement Works Better than Punishment

Fear and intimidation do not result in an efficient and motivated staff. In the short term you might get the attention you want from your employees, but in the long run they will be thinking about either how to get a new job or how to sabotage you. What's more, using fear as a management tactic is just plain lazy, a perceived shortcut to something that looks like respect but is something else altogether. It takes more time, focus, and commitment to manage without anger and/or negativity, but you will get more and better work out of your people. If you make it a point to criticize only in private, your staff will feel comfortable taking chances by sharing ideas at staff meetings, learning new skills, and volunteering for the more complicated projects. If you take notice when someone has gone the extra mile by praising them publicly, then you will soon have a team willing to work late to get assignments done. If you reward employees that help one another out, then you will be leading a unified group. If you are enthusiastic and positive about your job, the company, and your staff, they will feel it. This reinforcement and support will both energize and motivate your employees in a way that fear and intimidation just can't.

Running a Meeting

Too many meetings waste everyone's time. If a meeting is unstructured and undefined, it's a wasted opportunity to catch up and/or clarify. This is especially true of team meetings, where you have the attention of all of your people. There are a few tips for how to make the most of a meeting.

Have a reason

First and foremost, there should always be a genuine reason for a meeting. Don't just have one for the sake of it. If you want your staff to be engaged, then the topics for discussion should be specific and timely.

Be on time!

We've all had that power-tripping boss who strolls in 15 minutes after the meeting is to begin, getting off on the hushed audience. In addition to being rude, if your entire team is waiting for you to show up, you're wasting a serious number of people hours that could be spent being productive. This also holds true for employees who are constantly late. Everyone we spoke to gives the same advice about this management problem: start without them. Walking into a meeting that is already in progress will hopefully be so humiliating for your employee that he or she will make sure not to do it again.

Have an agenda

Meetings that become a stream-of-consciousness exercise are a waste of everyone's time. It's better to have worked out the topics and goals for the discussion well in advance. If you have a staff meeting coming up, then create the agenda and send it round a few days ahead of time so that your employees can come prepared. If you have a one-on-one with an employee scheduled, then write the discussion topics down on a piece of paper for your personal reference. Having an agenda is especially important when you are facing a delicate conversation with a member of your team. In uncomfortable situations, it is a possibility that the conversation will quickly veer off course, and you may find yourself talking about the weekend instead of their poor time-keeping. If you are meeting a potential customer or client, create the agenda at the office and review it just before the meeting. Planning what you are going to say in meetings large or small gives you control over the discussion and will help you to achieve the objectives of the meetings.

Take notes

When you are going over a project or goals that have assignments attached, it is helpful for everyone to have a written summary of the discussions. Assign one person to take notes in the meeting and e-mail them to everyone immediately after the meeting. Make sure you review the notes before they are circulated to ensure that they include everything you want them to.

Senior staff first

If you have a large departmental meeting, have a preliminary meeting with the senior members of the team to identify topics for discussion. If there are sensitive issues raised, then you want to prepare the top team for following up with their reports after the meeting. Caitlin worked for a publisher that was merging with another publisher. She and her colleagues were called into a company-wide pow-wow and told the news. Because the news was delicately delivered, and because immediately after the meeting the staff had one-on-ones with their managers, it was a smooth transition. It was obvious that senior people had been prepared, which made it better for everyone.

Put a lid on it

There are those individuals who love the sound of their own voice. Piping up whenever possible, they can disrupt even the best organized gathering. Since we are beyond the days of putting our hands up when we want attention, the louder, more aggressive members of the team tend to monopolize meetings, and it can be challenging for women to jump into the ring. But, as the manager, you need to move through the agenda and control the dialogue. Make it clear to those around the table when you want input and when you don't, by limiting the number of times you ask for participation. If someone interrupts you, look them in the eye and say, 'In a minute. I'm not quite finished.' Then, when you have finished, look back at the employee and give them permission to contribute, saying something along the lines of 'You had something to add?' It is all about maintaining control of the discussion.

Visual aids

Use visual aids only when necessary. Why? They slow down the proceedings, distract the participants, and take attention away from you. Although on an emotional level it might be comforting to have a PowerPoint presentation between you and those in front of you, it isn't always the best way to deliver your message.

Timing is everything

We've all experienced a meeting that was scheduled for an hour but stretched painfully into two. For the most part, long meetings are ineffective. By nature, we don't have the attention span to focus on anything for that length of time, especially if it isn't self-chosen. For team meetings try to stick to an hour, especially for brainstorms, where creativity often comes to a halt when people get tired. Take breaks if the meeting is going to stretch beyond two hours. Avoid scheduling meetings immediately after lunch, when people are often in a food coma. And, if you want the undivided attention of the group, don't have a meeting towards the end of the day, when the staff will be thinking about their journey home or getting to nursery or school on time to pick up their children

Opportunities abound

There are opportunities for professional growth in team gatherings. You could use the weekly meeting as a chance for your junior staff members to practise public speaking. We both worked for someone who had new people present something during each Monday morning meeting. You could ask senior members to lecture on their areas of expertise. For instance, if you manage a clothes shop, you could ask the buyer to present coming trends to the sales team.

Be the queen

For many women used to hanging back in public situations, leading meetings can be scary. Even today, after several years of running our own business and several more years of managing, it is a little intimidating to face a table full of people. You are on stage at these meetings, even if you are sitting down. But you need to embrace the role by sitting at the head of the table, projecting confidence, even if you don't feel it, and authoritatively running through the agenda. Whatever you do, don't let staff interrupt you, ever – it shows weakness – and keep reminding yourself that you 'own' this meeting.

Reach for the Stars: Setting Goals for Your People

What keeps you motivated as an employee? Is it the promotion on the horizon? Is it the next big client? Is it the personal challenge of mastering new skills such as public speaking, or will you simply not be satisfied until you have a corner office or become a partner? Whatever the motivation, there is *something* that keeps you going, and, since you have been promoted at some point to manager, then your employer has tapped into whatever it is that keeps you moving, looking forward, and contributing to the company's objectives. As a manager, you are responsible for using the team to achieve the goals of the company. The most efficient way to do this is by setting goals for your employees that will achieve the company's vision and at the same time tap into their needs and their vision for their career.

There are short-term and long-term goals for your employees. Short-term goals could include things like selling more of the blue T-shirts, writing the copy for the Bank Holiday weekend advertisement, baking 100 mince pies for the catering job, or ordering shipping supplies for a mailing. Long-term goals are usually those that merge the vision of the employee and the company, such as increasing sales of the T-shirt category by 20% over the summer, generating ideas for the Christmas ad campaign, creating new menu items for the catering company, developing a more efficient supply-ordering and shipping system.

Keys for establishing effective goals for your people include not setting too many. Goals need to be achievable, or you run the risk of undermining the confidence of your employee. The goal and the skills of the person to whom you assign it must be in synch. Always position the goal in the context of the company's aims: the company is expanding its line of casual wear, so the increase in the T-shirt sales is the first step; the catering business is often re-hired, and so it is essential to have a diverse selection of menu items to keep returning customers from getting bored; the company gets

10% off the cost of advertising in the local paper if they submit their copy early, and so writing the holiday text promptly will save money. Most importantly, you need to generate enthusiasm for and commitment to the goal, and so you want to paint it as an important part of your employee's professional development.

Good Witch or Big Bitch?

Your biggest fan
Here's a story from our friend Paige Perkins.

I dropped out of my career when I had my son Evan, but after three and a half years I was ready to dive back in. At the time, I was developing an interest in improving education but was uncertain about how to get into it. Ellen, the headmistress of an academy in Massachusetts, wanted me to work at her school. She was quite persistent, and, in part because of her reputation and belief in me, I agreed to come and work for her. After a year in the classroom and additional training, I became dean of this small but rapidly growing school. She was the absolutely best boss I have ever had. Beyond being a leader, she became a mentor for me.

Why do you think she was a Good Witch?
I've never known anyone who thought me more able than she. She had (and expressed, without being insincere in any way) tremendous belief in my ability to do my job, and she let me know it. I found that hugely energizing, and it made me willing to confront and do some very hard things.

Another thing is that she was smart and knew what she was doing in most areas; so, I knew I could rely on her judgment any time I decided to defer to her.

She was very clear about what her philosophy of education was, but she didn't force it on others. When push came to shove, she always stood up for what she believed in but would *always*, if I disagreed with her course of action, take the time to calmly and very thoroughly explain her viewpoint, so that I understood where she was coming from. Since she had the entire school to think about (finances, building, personnel, educational quality, etc.), whereas I had only part (the educational quality), I almost always came to understand her course of action once I had enough information.

While we had some big disagreements at times about how certain aspects of the school should run, she never pulled rank on me, ever. She always took the time to help me to understand a situation rather than just forcing me to do it her way.

Ellen tended to hire people to work for her who had a similar view of children and education. She was able to build a group of loving, cheerful people, whom she held together through strength of purpose. She was in communication with all of us at least once every couple of days. Each person was important to her, and she let them know it. At the same time, she held extremely high standards of organization, professionalism, etc. She always thought first about the survival of the school, because without it no one in the group would have anything. Then all the details followed.

She delegated responsibility, and I think this is one of the key points of a good boss. It's what made working under her such a joy for me. My job was mine, not hers. I could call all the shots. If I got stuck and didn't know what to do in a situation, she would help me. She never forced me to do anything.

She was willing to teach the people under her, in a very quiet way, so that they constantly got better and better at what they did. Then, at the same time, she could delegate more and more to them. This was, I believe, one of her most sterling qualities as a boss and one of the biggest keys to her success.

What did you learn from her?
I learned:

- that my instincts are good, and, if I just keep my cool, I can get a group of people to accomplish great things
- that solvency is absolutely essential to an organization if it is to survive, and that this is an area an executive has to constantly think about
- that good leadership is not necessarily showy, but it is accurate, caring, and ruthless about what's truly important
- that there is always something you can do, no matter what the situation. You just have to not lose your rag, but to calmly assess the entire situation, work out what it is you can do, and then carry it out. By the time you're done, you'll have already sorted out the next thing, and so on

Good Witch. Ellen didn't demonstrate any of the Bad Boss behaviour discussed in Chapter 4. She was confident, led by example, didn't micromanage, respected the team equally, set achievable goals and reasonable expectations, treated people professionally, and had faith in their abilities. But more than that, Ellen became something that only one in a million managers can become: a mentor. Paige, more than 20 years later, attributes much of her own success as a leader to what she learned working for Ellen at the academy. That is one Good Witch.

Direct and Indirect Reporting

If you find yourself in the unenviable position of having one of your staff treat their direct report badly, you are not alone. Dr Dorri Jacobs advises, 'In my experience, it is not a good idea to interfere unless you are asked for help from your direct report, or when you observe that a major problem exists. Otherwise the perception of those involved is that the manager has no real authority.' There is a very thin line between not interfering because you are respecting professional boundaries and being in collusion. If your direct report is beyond temperamental and leaning towards abusive, then you need to step in on behalf of the junior and the company. As a boss, it is your job to train your staff, and maybe your direct report needs to develop their own management skills.

Whenever possible, don't step in between two staff members. Ilene Rosen, a mediator with a busy practice in Manhattan, offers the following strategy. 'First discuss the problem with your direct report: explain why you are concerned, ask for his or her sense of what is going on and how best to resolve it, and if help would be appreciated. Get a time frame, if possible, for resolving the problem; thereafter meet to discuss the situation and check on progress. Support your direct report, rather than take over.'

Beware of letting your ego get in the way here. It can be a boost to be the good gal in these scenarios, but by stepping in as the hero you are just generating more work for yourself. When you undercut the authority of your direct subordinate, you are setting a precedent for staff to come to you with questions, issues, and problems. Taking care of someone else's support staff is far from your job. There is power that comes with your position, which you want to pass along to the people that directly report to you, not take it away.

No Chit-chat: A Guide to Getting the Most Out of Your Together Time

Unless you are unlikeable or off-putting in some way – and we doubt that – then the chances are that your employees will want to chat with you – a lot, as much as possible, and for a variety of reasons. Maybe they feel the need to bond; maybe they are trying to get in with you; maybe they are lonely; maybe they need to sound off; or maybe they are just highly sociable. Whatever the reason, you don't have that much extra time available for non-productive chit-chat. Even if you are swamped, keeping your door closed is not an option, because you don't want to alienate your team. You also want your employees to feel comfortable talking to you about company issues, and staying unavailable won't foster that kind of environment.

Sometimes there is more behind the chit-chat. There are those who are uncomfortable with face-to-face discussions and ramble rather than tackle an issue. What's the solution? Give everyone a few minutes where you are completely focused on what they are saying. During their few minutes, don't check your e-mail, answer the phone, or peruse your diary. Think of it as their time. If they just needed to say their piece, then you heard them. If they wanted to bond with you, then you gave them a little of that. And, if there is something more going on, you can pursue it. When their few minutes are over, gracefully end the conversation, trying not to be too abrupt or you may undo the good feelings you have generated.

Girl Talk: Diane Bates

Diane Bates co-founded Blue Sky Communications seven years ago. As the president of this busy public relations business, she has had the opportunity to manage employees at all levels. With an enviable 0% staff turnover rate, Diane is clearly an excellent leader. In this Girl Talk, she shares the secret of her success.

What do you get out of managing on a personal and professional level?
Management is my favourite part of the job, especially as a business owner with 20 years' experience in my field. It gives me a chance to cultivate new talent and to teach people things I have learned in my career. Further, I've been managed by some individuals who were great at their job but poor managers, as well as by some fantastic managers, and I've spent a lot of time considering the differences between the two. Specifically, what they did or didn't do to motivate me, teach me, inspire me, and help me stay excited about work. Management in itself is a fascinating study in human behaviour, and, by simply relying on a substructure of principles – respect, honesty, communication, clarity of direction, the ability to recognize inherent strengths and weaknesses in different personalities, etc. – it can be easy and fun to groom people for success in their careers.

How have you evolved as a leader?
When we start out we operate mostly as tacticians and then as leaders later on; so in the beginning I was more concerned with how well I performed in my job and the tasks in hand. But what I didn't know at the time was that my managerial

skills were being cultivated by those managing me. Only in hindsight did those experiences, good and bad, come in handy. For example, I was repeatedly asked by a former boss to tend to her dog (walk him, feed him, babysit him, etc.) – she brought him to work every day. It seemed funny at first, but after a while it really undermined my self-respect at work. In fact, any time I was asked to run a personal errand for any boss I did it with a smile, but I had an inherent understanding of the fact that it was simply wrong and showed a total lack of respect for me as a human being. Certainly, this is standard operating procedure in the food chain of corporate America, but it is something I never do with my staff. No one in my office handles personal chores for me. I'd be embarrassed even to ask them to!

An example of how good management influenced me was with a fabulous supervisor I once had who was amazing at deflecting the glory of success to her team. She was the first to attribute our collective successes or jobs well done to her 'fabulous team' and never hogged the accolades for herself. It was incredibly motivating for me, and, as a result, I never hog the glory or accolades now; in fact, I really couldn't care less about that. But my staff being motivated – now that I care about, because it means we will do good work, have low turnover, offer clients continuity, and all those good things that come from a happy staff. That impacts on me and the business in a far bigger, more important way than any pat on the shoulder will. I know the accolades mean a lot more to our staff; so, as far as I am concerned, they can have all the glory. It only makes our agency – and me, too – look great by association. That's why it's so important for managers to be aware of the impact their style will have on junior people as they rise in the ranks.

I have evolved as a leader through years of experience and having poor managers. I have also learned over time that one must always consider the ultimate best and worst possible outcomes of a situation and attempt to steer it towards the positive. This sometimes means your staff does not see, understand, or agree with some of the decisions you make, but, in business, one must always protect the business entity first, otherwise there will *be* no managers or employees.

Tips for being a good and effective manager?

- Be accountable.
- We're all equal. All people, regardless of their position in their job, deserve and need to be heard, to feel respected, and to have their individual talents and gifts celebrated.
- Get to know them really well. At my agency we measure our employees' performance based on their individual talents, not on some generic corporate template.
- Understand your influence. Many managers are unaware of the impact their management style will have on junior people as they grow professionally.
- Rely on a foundation of principles like respect, honesty, communication, and clarity of direction, and trust your own ability to recognize inherent strengths and weaknesses in different personalities.

7

Playing Goddess: Evaluations, Promotions, and Giving the Chop

Remember all those evaluations you had to sit through over the years, your mouth shut tight while your superior listed all your shortcomings in clear, concise, and easy-to-decipher language? Well, now it's your turn to give the reviews, promotions, and, yes, occasionally even notice.

Evaluations can be a great learning experiences, for both you and your employees. They allow you to establish the big picture for each person on your staff and provide an opportunity to re-energize the employee and discuss her professional goals. If you want to get the inside scoop on what your employees really think of your job performance, let them turn the tables and put you to the test.

Promotions and pay rises are often the best part of being a bigwig, because they offer the rare opportunity to be the good gal. On the other hand, you might find, as many bosses do, that the hardest part of your job is deciding what to do when someone just is not working out. It can be tough, but, if you follow the advice we offer in the section entitled *Got to Go* (page 144), you will survive and avoid traumatizing the surviving members of your team.

This chapter will give you the low-down on performance reviews (what to do and what *not* to do, as well as a sample performance evaluation form); how to turn bad news into good vibes; how to give (and get) constructive criticism; and how to let people down gently when they don't quite cut the mustard.

Day-to-day Performance Monitoring and Feedback

If you were ever surprised by something raised during one of your reviews, you probably had a bad manager. Supervising another person is about the everyday flow of work. It is also about the tone and energy of the team. It stands to reason that to pay proper respect to both of those aspects, you need to manage a little everyday. Jennifer Kyle, a VP at a culinary publication, tells us, 'There are many scheduled internal and external meetings, but I also like to be available just to get things done more quickly without creating an unnecessary process.' To open the doors of communication, start by touching base with your employees at least once a day and take the time to get to know a little about them. We had a boss who would sweep through the office in the morning without even a smile for those of us sitting in the 'pit'. At the end of the day, it left us feeling used, replaceable, and unappreciated and not like the precious resources we were.

Because it is your job to keep the flow of work moving along, when people come to you with questions, you should answer them as quickly as possible. If you don't have the answer at your fingertips, then get back to them later in the day or let them know when to expect an answer. This also applies to reviewing documents. As a manager you most likely have a stack of reports, presentations, articles and/or reviews sitting on your desk waiting for your changes or approval. Don't let them gather dust; people will either think it is okay for them to procrastinate or they will feel disrespected by you. Worse, if you are putting off changes, then you are stopping the flow of work and impeding those who report to you from doing their job.

If you are regularly making contact, you will also become aware of the things that are not getting done sooner rather than later. If you notice a task perpetually on an employee's to-do list, ask why. Your person may need more direction, another set of skills, or perhaps just a motivational nudge. This kind of daily monitoring, which we hasten to point out is not the same as micromanaging, will give you more control over what is getting done and when, and in turn a real sense of mastery over the workplace.

Make it your long-term goal not to bring up any new issue in the review with each of your employees. Instead, you should be letting them know whether or not they have succeeded in addressing any issue that you have already brought to their attention at the moment you noticed it. Not only does this avoid melodramatic reviews, but it is also a more effective means of managing: people are more apt to understand and respond to constructive criticism if it's presented at the time of the mistake, when the memory of what they did wrong is still fresh in their mind.

Why Appraisals Are a Must
As an employee, you probably dreaded your performance appraisal. Now, as a manager, you probably dread it in a different way as you face your stacks of filled-in appraisal forms. We not only want to encourage you to embrace the appraisal process but we want you to consider doing it more often. The standard annual

appraisal gives you and your staff only one opportunity to set goals together, share feedback from clients and those above, tackle performance issues, and reiterate their role in the company's objectives. We worked for a company that had four appraisals a year, and only one was a salary review. This constant checking-in opened up communications between the manager and her staff. Sharon Rose, the owner of several clothing stores, says, 'Without useful feedback, developmental needs, and a plan, it is very difficult to keep people motivated and make sure everyone is working with the same intentions.'

Ideally, the evaluation should set out to review the quality of work, communicate the expectations of the company, and open up discussions about the employee's own career goals. If you are planning on firing the employee, then the review also provides a formal documentation of their shortcomings and fireable offences. Conducting an honest review is crucial; if you sack someone after giving a glowing review, you are opening yourself up to a charge of wrongful dismissal.

Good Witch or Big Bitch?

Fair and balanced

Chrisi Colabella of CIS is one of our mentors. She built her company from scratch and now has 34 employees in three states. She's read all of the management books, gone to training sessions, and, through years of trial and error, she's developed into an inspiring manager. She maintains a professional relationship with her staff and doesn't focus her energy on getting people to like her. She's fair, she listens to her staff, and she tries to help them to achieve their potential. And guess what? They like her – they really like her.

Chrisi does career development plans and performance reviews with all of her employees. Here she outlines her programme for us.

- Each employee has a written, clearly defined job description that I review with them two to three times per year. At these mini-reviews we go over strengths and weaknesses and discuss ways for them to improve. We also discuss their ambitions within the company.
- At the annual review, if they receive a bad report, I feel that I have been totally fair and justified in the evaluation. And I don't feel like a bitch, because they know what is expected of them and how they have been performing throughout the entire process.
- We then set a plan for what each person wants to achieve in the coming year, as well as what I want them to achieve. This is the goal plan we use for the mini-reviews, and the process starts all over again.
- I taught my operations manager how to do the same process with her direct reports. Together we go through each written review before her meetings so that she's comfortable with the system.

Sample Appraisal

At our company, YC Media, we have instituted a 'begin', 'end', 'save', and 'track' appraisal system – what we refer to as BEST. These four elements are summarized for each employee and provide both the starting points and framework for the discussion. We like to give appraisals twice a year, but only one is devoted to pay rises. The other is focused entirely on productivity and goal setting. During this non-salary review, we also ask the employees to write up a performance evaluation of *our* management. While some might baulk at this, we have found that, more than anything else, it gives us a better idea of how the employees like to be managed. We have included one of our reviews below. (Don't worry we made a few changes; we don't want to embarrass any of our staff members!)

Begin

First, we discuss three actions that we want the employee to start doing. We tie the *begin* actions to either short- or long-term goals for the employee. Again, these statements are a jumping off point for a longer dialogue about what we want to start seeing from our employee.

For example:

- attending more industry events
- speaking up in team meetings
- long-term planning for clients

End

Next, we raise three actions or habits we want the employee to stop, sooner rather than later. We try not to include the really small foibles or ticks that drive us crazy, but focus instead on bringing up issues that are serious enough to warrant 100% focus of both the manager and her employee. The *ends* should be actions that directly affect her ability to grow in her career.

For example:

- missing deadlines
- putting off difficult jobs
- delegating time-sensitive tasks to her assistant

Save

In this section, we discuss three actions that we want the employee to keep doing. When we get to this section of the review we sigh with relief because we have all got through some tough issues. Again, we try to keep the focus on the big stuff here, because hopefully we have been pointing out good work on a weekly, if not a daily, basis. So these are the action points that will get them a promotion and/or a pay rise down the road.

For example:

- her creative input on client proposals
- her attention to detail
- the quality of her writing

Track

These actions outline a plan for the employee to track their growth in the *begin* section of the review. They also spell out what success looks like to us: 'We want you to begin A, so if we see B you have succeeded'. Since the *track* items are a starting point for the discussion, we then work together with the employee on achieving these goals.

For example:

- attend two industry events a year
- contribute one comment per team meeting
- show me your proposed campaigns for each client so that I can help you, if you need me to, with the planning

Five Common Evaluation Mistakes
Not enough specific examples

Both positive and negative review statements have more impact when backed up by specific examples. 'You tend to miss deadlines' is easier to dismiss than 'You have a habit of missing deadlines. Last month the new business proposal I asked you to draft for Soy Yogurt wasn't on my desk until four days after it was due to reach the potential client. June's status report wasn't delivered until the middle of July, and your final edits to the Black Raspberry Jam press release were two days late.' If you put criticisms in a context during the review it will force the employee to think twice about their past and future performance. Likewise, positive reviews, when backed up by specific examples, help to motivate your staff. 'Your clients all seem to like you,' is nice to hear, but wouldn't it be better to say 'I have had many calls from the marketing directors at Regent Restaurant Group and Wellbeing Spa both telling me how thrilled they are with your results.'

Goals are too vague

If you set a goal for a sales rep to 'increase sales', that is open to interpretation, but if you tell her that you want to see a 5% increase, there is no disputing whether or not it's been achieved.

No context

To help develop your employee's big picture thinking, review all of the roles she has in the company. She needs to know that while keeping customers happy is a crucial part of her job, as is also being a mentor for her direct report. While she does need to be focused on the sales goals for the Main Street Clothing Store, she also needs to start being tuned into the company's overall sales goals.

Too negative

If you bombard someone with criticism, two things will happen: they will stop hearing you, and, out of self-preservation, they will convince themselves that you are wrong. We recommend that, if you are reviewing someone you want to keep and develop, you keep your criticisms brief and concise. Balance criticisms with good news, while providing action steps for fixing the problems. Reassure them that you are committed to turning it around with them.

Too positive

It is easier to deliver good news, but, if you spend the review patting the backs of your employees, then you are missing an opportunity to help to push them to the next level. If you are not sharing with your subordinate the roadmap to a promotion, you are robbing them of their professional development.

A True Mentor

Abigail Disney, founder and president of the Daphne Foundation, told us this story.

The best manager I have ever met is Gerry Laybourne, formerly of Nickolodeon and then Disney, now of Oxygen Media. She has built an empire of devotedly loyal employees who would lie down on the train tracks for her because of a rule that in many other places would be totally radical: she is the queen of nice. She is nice to waiters and cleaners and secretaries and senators and princes and little old ladies on the bus. She is absolutely adamant about the power of niceness, and she is walking proof that, as a life strategy, not only does it work, but it creates an aura of contentment and clarity around the person who practises it and everyone around them. It is an extraordinary thing, and brave, since this is not a doctrine supported by most of those in the Fortune 500. She is a hero.

The Good News: Turning Bad News Into Better Employees

Let's say that one of your event planners is loved by the clients but has a gruff manner with outside contractors and that results in complaints from the caterer, the florist, and the band. Even if they begin raising their fees when she is on the case, it would be better to keep her and work through her challenges. Rather than wait until review time to address the issue, you should jump right in by setting up a one-to-one with her. Begin the discussion by providing the event planner with an overview of the problem, using specific examples to back it up. Juli Tolleson, a director at US Concepts-Diageo Wine & Spirits, would then ask for her 'perspective on the project; then explain clearly and constructively what could have been done to make it more effective. I also ask what I can do better in the future to support her so that she can do a better job'. When good employees go bad, there is usually a reason for it, and often it is a simple case of not having what they need to get the job done. Sarah Barns, a sales representative for a computer company, tells us that sometimes the hard talks can turn things around with a disappointing employee. 'I had a junior-level employee who really shone in the interview process and then fell apart quickly after starting. We realized it about three months into her employment and figured we would let her go, but gave her a warning and continued through a full warning process, and honestly never thought she could turn it around. But she did. Apparently she needed more direction than we realized and talking everything out really helped.'

Got to Go: When Good News Isn't Good Enough

Unfortunately you will have to fire people, and, even if they are the worst employee ever, firing anyone is a nightmare. Janie Kleiman, senior vice president of television production for 20th Century Fox Television, concurs: 'The only aspect of my position that I don't find enjoyable is when an employee has to be replaced. We are all dependent on our jobs to support our families . . . Some people need their jobs, as their jobs identify who they are and have become part of their personality. I take it very seriously when I have to fire or replace someone.'

The bad news is that it is part of your job; so – no excuses – you must wield the axe. It would be best for both of you if the employee resigns; so indicate at the verbal warning stage that things are not looking good, and then at the written stage reiterate that the situation is looking dire. Concrete examples of mistakes will close the door to a discussion. At this point, hopefully, the employee will take the hint and pack her bags. It is far less ugly if they give their notice. If, however, they refuse, fail to be realistic, and don't change, then you are going to have to do it for them. Firing someone is one situation as a manager that will forever cast you – in that person's mind at least – as a bitch. The best you can hope to do is to retain your dignity and treat your soon-to-be-ex-employee with respect. Invite them into your office, sit them down, list the reasons you are firing them by reading from past reviews and warnings, and ask them to leave the building that day. Why should they leave that day? Because they could become destructive or cause the remaining team to feel anxious, guilty, resentful, or fearful. This is where it can get really messy, because they will need to be escorted out. Check with HR because you might have to enlist the security department to accompany the ex-employee out of the door, with only a pit stop at their desk to grab personal belongings. They will need to leave any and everything that belongs to your company.

To make this as easy as possible for all concerned, don't give the employee an opportunity to be emotional. If you apologize for what you have to do or wait for her to let you off the hook by telling you it is OK, then you are leaving room for her to cry, scream, or throw something. Another way to make sure it doesn't escalate is by giving honest feedback along the way so that you are not surprising her with anything new. Deliver the news quickly and succinctly, and don't take responsibility for things turning sour. If you did your job right and offered suggestions and methods for solving the problems, then she owns this, not you. 'I fire someone when I have warned them and given them a chance to save themselves, but they either don't have the ability to do the job or they just don't care enough. There are too many good, hard working, smart people to have any mediocre people around,' says promotions director, Frances Miller.

If you feel at all unsure about the legal aspects of letting someone go, don't act without taking advice. If your organization has an HR department, use it. If you run your own business and you don't have an HR department, visit the government's Business Link site (www.businesslink.gov.uk) for information on this issue. There are statutory procedures in place in the United Kingdom relating to dismissals, and it's important that you follow them closely at all times.

Disciplined Disciplinarian: Being Consistent, Fair, and Constructive

Mistakes are always a learning opportunity for both you and your employees, so make the best of the discussion you will inevitably be having with your subordinate. Set aside a time to speak to your person as soon as the mistake happens. Outline beforehand the points you want to make and specific suggestions for how the task or situation could have been handled better. During the meeting be calm, clear, and unemotional. After you have presented the issue, listen to what she has to say. Is she pointing out challenges that are affecting her ability to do her job? Does she need additional training? Is she just unwilling to accept responsibility? If she seems willing to work on it and is onboard with making changes, then work with her to create a clear list of steps to turn the problem around.

When Good People Leave

Prepare yourself, because it's going to happen, and you can't take it personally. Good employees will outgrow you at some point, be recruited, or want your job. Leah Andrews, a restaurant manager, said, 'I knew what was happening as soon as Cheri asked if she could come into my office and proceeded to shut the door behind her. All I wanted to do was fall on the floor, scream "Noooo!" and cry like a baby.' Any manager knows what a blow it is when a great person leaves. It affects the equilibrium of the team, since everyone was in a groove of working together. It puts more work on the plates of several of the team members, including the manager. There is the pressure to hire someone 'just like them' or at the very least find someone great right away. It distracts you and several members of the group from meeting their goals. Also, on an emotional level, if you cared about the employee, you will miss her. Unfortunately (and fortunately) there are just too many opportunities these days for people to stay long at any one company.

If you think that she is worth fighting for, then by all means give it a go. Check with HR and *your* boss about what you can counter-offer in salary and/or promotion. That said, you should also be aware that counter-offers are not always appreciated. How many times did you give notice only to be told that the company 'really wants to keep you', and suddenly your supervisor had the funds to pay you more? How did that make you feel? It makes most of us really angry, but not as angry as no counter-offer would make us. So, do the dance and offer more, but don't expect it to work.

The best you can do is prepare yourself for the likelihood of it happening at some point. It behoves you to think ahead and plan for each strong employee's departure by staying in the loop, having at least a basic understanding of their job responsibilities, and preparing yourself mentally for the possibility of doing much more work yourself until you find a replacement. If your staff works directly with accounts, then commit yourself to some face-to-face time with each of the accounts, so that in the event of their usual contact leaving they will still feel taken care of by a representative of the company. If one of your key employees works in shifts, make sure that you have a plan for juggling schedules should she no longer be available. If she travels to attend trade shows or conferences, then come to terms with the fact that you might have to go on the road at some point until a replacement can be found.

Boy Talk: David Craig

David Craig, director Drama Programming, A&E Television, has worked for six high-powered women during his career. Being successful while navigating the competitive waters of the entertainment business is not easy. We spoke to him about his experiences working for women.

Tell us about any common challenges you noticed your female bosses dealing with in the workplace and how they overcame them.

The common challenge seems to be their interactions with men in positions above them, especially if the man is less qualified than they are for the position. This still seems to happen frequently in business, even in TV and film, and it is very frustrating, and the usual response is to remain professional and operate as if this were not the case. The interesting thing that I have not encountered is much struggle that these women have balancing their work and home lives. They can maybe afford to hire home help, have kids already off to school or grown, or somehow manage to handle both aspects of their lives without sacrificing their ambitions at work.

Do you think women or men make better bosses?

The answer is mixed. Because I've had strong relationships with women in my family, I've tended to feel that I could work better with women and felt more supportive towards them as they made their way in male-driven industries. That said, I've had the misfortune of working with some of the most ruthless, competitive, and non-supportive women in both film and publishing. One of the things I found difficult was expecting a more compassionate or sensitive approach towards people management, which has backfired. In many cases, the more difficult women bosses worked very hard to eliminate any softer side to their management. In my opinion, they were trying to overcompensate for being pitted against men in higher positions; however, these same women had no qualms about exploiting their sex appeal to get favours or benefits from men. This has always struck me as a contradiction in a political sense of women's rights. What these tougher and more successful women (both the better and worse bosses) have taught me is that the work environment is not about gender politics and they do not want to be seen as role models. For them, business is war and all is fair in war and work.

Are there any female/boss character traits that worked well for you?
For those bosses who were more supportive and less threatened by me, I've been able to grow as an employee and help build the company more successfully than if I had been held back. In exchange, I've willingly offered more loyalty and support, which has resulted in a couple of long-term jobs working for these more supportive female bosses. Their support proved mutually beneficial.

Did you have a favorite female boss?
I've actually had two great female bosses. One was film producer, Marcia Nasatir, who, despite 40 years seniority,

treated me as an equal from the first day and allowed me to participate in all aspects of the company. The other great boss was television executive, Delia Fine, who has helped me enormously with navigating the waters in my first corporate position and helped me to use my strengths to better advantage.

Culture Is Queen: The Lowdown on Corporate Culture

Corporate culture is the heart and soul of an organization and guides how employees act and feel. It comprises values, ethics, and aesthetics. Company values, dress code, phone manners, and benefits policies all fall under the umbrella, and a corporate culture can be stated or understood. For example, YC Media has a very casual office dress code, yet it's understood by all of our employees that when outside guests or clients are coming in then everyone must dress up for the occasion.

Corporate culture can be prescribed from the beginning or evolve over time. It generally reflects the founder's ethos but adapts as a company matures and grows. Of course the animators at The Walt Disney Company stopped wearing jackets and ties to work every day, but the company still stays true to the core mission that Walt himself began of providing quality entertainment for people around the world.

Dr Randall Hansen, webmaster of Quintessential Careers, is also publisher of its electronic newsletter, *QuintZine*. He writes a biweekly career advice column under the name The Career Doctor. He believes that assessing how well you will fit into a corporate culture will be a strong indicator of your happiness and success in a job. On his website, he recommends that you interview other employees in a company to get a real picture of the culture. Dr Hansen's questions are worth considering when interviewing for a new position or assessing your own corporate culture.

- Which ten words would you use to describe your company?
- What's it really like to work here? Do you like it here?
- What's really important?
- How are employees valued?
- What skills and characteristics does the company value?
- Do you feel as though you know what is expected of you?
- How do people from different departments interact?
- Are there opportunities for further training and education?
- How do people get promoted?
- What behaviour gets rewarded?
- Do you feel as though you know what's going on?
- How effectively does the company communicate to its employees?

What Defines Your Corporate Culture? Balancing Standards and Style

We all want the perfect workplace – a bright, happy environment full of productive and motivated workers whistling while they work. Creating and maintaining such a place requires thought and discipline. At the heart of happy companies are happy people. Creating a culture dedicated to employee happiness is one way to ensure success, and it starts with some basic premises. Pay people fairly, if not better than the industry standard. Create a benefits package that takes all the worker's needs into consideration. Be clear about goals for the company and individuals and communicate with them on a regular basis.

Most of the women we interviewed acknowledged that their corporate culture and management style work hand-in-hand. Gretchen Monahan, owner of six Grettacole salons and spas in the Boston area, described her 110 employees as a family, and talked about how they support her and she supports them. Claire Burke, senior vice president at Hunter Public Relations in New York City, explained how people in her organization who care more about their job title than their job responsibilities won't last. 'My clients don't even know my title,' she said. 'My team always roll their eyes when we're in a meeting and the client introduces me as their account supervisor. But for senior management, getting the work done is the priority, not throwing around our titles and position.'

Company values shouldn't be just lip service, but the guiding philosophy that employees know and integrate into their working lives. Not surprisingly, the best companies to work for do this the best. Wegman's chain of supermarkets was voted the number one company to work for in 2005 by *Fortune* magazine because of its unusual mission: 'Employees first, customers second'. The Wegman family's rationale has always been when employees are happy, customers will be too. And they put their money where their mouth is: they pay their staff more than their competition, and, in an industry characterized by either strong unions or no benefits at all, healthcare is offered to all employees, part-time and full-time.

To determine which companies are best, *Fortune* magazine has developed a four-part evaluation that contributes to one-third of the overall score. We think it is a good matrix to use when evaluating your own culture. *Fortune* looks at credibility (communication with employees); respect (opportunities and benefits); fairness (compensation, diversity); and pride/camaraderie (philanthropy, celebrations).

How do you want your employees to feel when they walk through the door? How do you communicate with your employees? Does everyone 'feel the touch' of senior management? Are opportunities for growth and benefits competitive with or better than the industry standard? Is your workplace fair? Do you pay people the same as or better than the industry standard? Is your workplace diverse, including people from all different backgrounds? Does it make employee career development a priority? Does the company make philanthropy a priority? Does it care about more than its own bottom line?

Only when you have considered all of these questions and put a positive workplace culture in place can you be assured that your good employees won't leave as soon as a better opportunity comes along.

What Do You Stand for?

Assessing, articulating, and then living your brand values will be challenging. It will also be the most important thing a company can do to create a consistent culture in which its team can thrive. At YC Media, we value client service above all else. Having created a laid-back but professional workplace, we champion individuality and offer work-hard-and-the-sky's-the-limit career opportunities.

Most corporate websites state the company's mission and values. We read through a number of them when researching this chapter and our favorite by far is Yahoo!'s; see for yourself at http://docs.yahoo.com/info/values/.

Keep in mind that you are not the only one thinking about values. Potential employees are thinking about them too. As a matter of fact, university career counsellors suggest that job candidates assess their own values before seeking employment. The career board website of the University of New South Wales in Sydney, Australia suggests that students make a list of values that are important to them, and offer samples. They suggest students look at extrinsic values including wealth, power and prestige, security, status, recognition, and perks and bonuses; intrinsic values such as achievement, honesty, compassion, ambition, and personal and intellectual growth; contextual values like organization size, indoors or outdoors, aesthetically pleasing, varied versus same; and people issues including teamwork and independence.

The Word: Tessa Jane Graham, Founding Partner

Tessa Jane Graham is a founding partner of Fresh Partners (www.fresh-partners.com), a company dedicated to developing personality-led brands and businesses. Fresh Partners grew from the work Tessa did with celebrity chef Jamie Oliver as the director of strategic development. Under her leadership, Jamie's business expanded to 46 countries and 23 languages and has sold over 12 million books worldwide. Her experience developing global brands includes previous stints with Joe Boxer, Red Sheriff, and Razorfish, the digital consultancy, where she worked with a variety of global clients. She's been based in Canada and the United States, and is currently in the United Kingdom, where she is a brand consultant. Tessa shares her experience in developing a corporate culture, managing her team, and managing the trials and tribulations of a new business.

- As a branding person, I feel that understanding an organisation's brand is key to being able to be a good manager. If everyone on the team understands the vision and the mission, as well as the role that they can have in reaching these goals, everyone is focused in the same direction. Done right, the brand influences everything that the company does, most importantly its corporate culture. The team then understands what their common goal is, and everyone, ideally, works towards it.

● I've always thought that transparency in management is best practice. Sharing with the team where things are, what could be better, what the numbers look like, how people are feeling – this way there are no secrets and no hidden agendas. Everything is out in the open.

Casual Friday: Why a Dress Code Works

Cynthia Rowley is an acclaimed fashion designer with stores all round the world. With writer Ilene Rosenzweig, she is also the creator of *Swell*, a national lifestyle brand. She has a strict dress-code for new employees and interns that was developed after one too many run-ins with bad outfits and bare midriffs. After all, one person's personal style can become your nightmare.

In her book *Creating We: Change I-Thinking to WE-Thinking and Build a Healthy, Thriving Organization*, Judith Glaser tells a story of her experience with the Donna Karan dress code policy when she was consulting for them.

'In 1996, the day before my first visit to Donna Karan International to meet Donna and her senior leadership team, I spent a lot of time thinking about and planning what I would wear. At the time I did not own one piece of her line of clothing, although I would have loved to. I would buy designer clothes only when they were on sale, and I did not have a favourite designer. From time to time, I shopped at designer outlets to find my "status apparel", which I proudly wore to appropriate parties. While I almost became a designer out of high school, that was long ago. My design instincts for apparel had given way to my instincts for helping executives create the future of their businesses, and I was okay with the trade-off, until I met Donna Karan and her 31 senior executives.

The suit I chose for my first visit was quite beautiful: taupe and white wool with an Italian designer's name on the label – someone I never bought from before, or after. It had a Chanel look, and, in my mind, I was dressed appropriately for the occasion.

As the door opened, I got the shock of my life. It took a few seconds to fully sink in. There I stood – all alone – in my beautiful taupe suit, surrounded by two dozen executives all wearing black – black suits, black trousers, black tops.'

Judith later found out that Donna required everyone to wear black, because other colours impinged upon her creativity. She wanted a monochromatic back-drop to design. Not knowing the dress code put Judith at a disadvantage; her outfit screamed 'outsider' as she walked through the door.

But a dress code isn't just about fashion and for people in the fashion business. It's about fitting in, being appropriate, and representing. Styles of dress change from business to business and city to city. Frankly, a clearly defined dress code would be a relief from the many hours of outfit anxiety we've both shared trying to decide what to wear to a big meeting, presentation, or on the first day at a new job. When Kim was at her first job in New York City, she had no appropriate clothes – only she didn't know it until years later, when a group of people had got together to laugh about old times. Her 'business-girl' outfits got the biggest chuckle – more specifically, the fuschia rayon trouser suit with a matching scarf and straw hat (give her a break; it was 1990, and she's from New Jersey). What worked when she was a sales associate at the Casual Corner in Colorado most definitely didn't work in the halls of a design magazine in New York City. So, how do you define a reasonable dress code policy?

The American Small Business Association's online Women's Business Center (www.onlinewbc.gov) offers guidelines for employee dress code and sample language for your employee handbook: 'As an employee of XYZ, we expect you to present a clean and professional appearance when you represent us, whether that is in, or outside of, the office. Management, sales personnel, and those employees who come in contact with our public are expected to dress in accepted corporate tradition. A specific list of suggested dos and definite don'ts, including a detailed definition of business casual, is available from your personnel representative and will be posted in each work area.

It is just as essential that you act in a professional manner and extend the highest courtesy to co-workers, visitors, customers, vendors, and clients. A cheerful and positive attitude is essential to our commitment to extraordinary customer service and impeccable quality.'

But is that helpful? What is 'accepted corporate tradition'? Make it easy for your team and yourself. Be as specific as possible. Never say, 'Please dress up, we have to meet a new client tomorrow.' Instead be specific: 'suits' or 'no blue jeans'. If you're a small enough organization, do what we do: recommend a specific outfit of theirs that you've noticed and that would be appropriate for the occasion.

In the absence of a clearly defined dress code, pay attention. What do your superiors wear? Think about where you're going and who you're going to see. Nothing zaps your confidence faster than being accused of being (or feeling) inappropriately dressed.

The Dress Code That Goes Everywhere

To save agonizing (and embarrassment), we've created the dress code that goes everywhere.

- When in doubt, wear black. A black trouser suit, a black dress, a black skirt with any kind of top works everywhere for every occasion. Throw in some black shoes; without even thinking, you're perfect.

- Natural fibres always. Stay away from anything shiny. With wool and cotton you can never go wrong.
- Grooming goes a long way. Get a regular manicure or do it yourself. Keep your eyebrows waxed, threaded, or plucked. Keep hair split-end free, and, when overdue for a haircut or colour, just pull it back into a ponytail.
- Shoes make the woman, and there's a pair to fit any size – something you cannot say about expensive designer jeans. Keep your shoes in good condition. Get soles and heels repaired and keep them polished, especially boots.
- No bare midriffs, ever. We love tank tops and hate tummies.
- Unless you've got the legs, save the mini-skirts for the weekend.
- Wear day clothes during the day and evening clothes at night. We worked with a woman who wore taffeta skirts with matching shoes and halter tops to work and we could never work out if she hadn't gone home the night before.
- Check the magazines. We love *In Style*'s fashion coverage. They give you a number of options for all shapes, sizes, and budgets.
- Wear make-up; you will look better. It doesn't have to be heavy; just a little foundation, blusher, and mascara will do the trick.

Starting From Scratch: Challenges and Opportunities for the Entrepreneur

It's really exciting when you start a new business – there's nothing but upside. You can create the kind of culture you always wanted to work in. It's your party now, and (if you're lucky) no one will be crying. Here's a list of questions to ask when starting up.

- How am I going to communicate with my employees and how often?
- What is their office space going to look like?
- How much does the competition pay for the same job?
- What kinds of benefits does the competition offer?

- What does the company value, and how are you going to communicate it to the team?

A Look Through Johari's Window

Wading through management teachings, we occasionally stumble on some theory that seems interesting enough to break down and share.

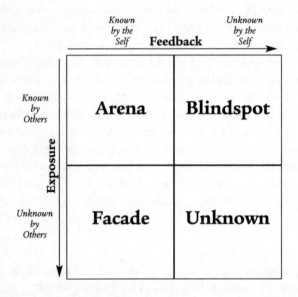

The Johari Window is a tool that management consultants use to help to increase communication within organizations. It was created by Joe Luft and Harry Ingham at the University of California in the 1950s. Their 'window' offers a way of looking at how communication is expressed. Simply put, the window reflects the interaction of information between self and others. Good communication happens in the top left quadrant, known as the *arena*, the area that is 'known by self' and 'known by others'. Below the *arena* is the *facade*, the quadrant where you know, but others don't. The quadrant next to the *arena* is the *blindspot*, where others know about you, but you don't. And below the *blindspot* is the *unknown*, the quadrant where neither you nor others know.

Their assumption is that productivity and interpersonal effectiveness are directly related to the amount of information that is shared between you and others. For example, if a manager knows that a member of her team has just relocated from another country, and the team member knows that communication is different in her new country, then the chances are that they will work together to try to understand each other before jumping to conclusions.

Your goal (without sharing unnecessary personal information, of course) is to make the *arena* as large as possible. The larger the *arena* becomes, the more rewarding, effective, and productive the relationship can be. You can increase the size of the arena by regular and honest exchange of feedback, and a willingness to disclose personal feelings. People around you will understand what makes you tick and what you find easy or difficult to do, and they can provide appropriate support. And, of course, you can do the same for them.

Increasing the size of the arena

Influencing the size of the *arena* is in your control. The more you share relevant information you have with others, the more you enlarge the *arena* in a downward direction, reducing the *facade*. Luft and Ingham call this the *exposure process* and it requires open and candid expression of feelings and facts.

It takes two to communicate, and the other party must also *expose* (share information) in order for communication to be productive. Therefore, you must actively solicit information from others. Luft and Ingham call this *feedback solicitation*. As you receive feedback, the *arena* extends to the right, reducing your *blindspot*.

To establish effective communication, you need to engage in *exposure* and *feedback solicitation* – give information and ask questions of others. It's all in your control, and, as the manager, it's your responsibility to increase the *arena*. When Sarilee Norton was a senior vice president at Tenneco Packaging, she would schedule a quarterly meeting to review goals and objectives. She told us, 'Getting people to use their brains – intellect, creativity, sensitivity – at the same time drawing them in on a personal level can really have an impact. I used to do a quarterly lunch and ask each participant to do something that would give the group insight into the individual and what motivated them. For example, one lunch I asked each person to bring an object from their past that would reveal something we probably didn't know about them. For example, Barb, my secretary, brought her ballet shoes and clippings from when she danced semi-professionally. None of us knew she was a dancer. Then each person would talk about the projects they were working on, what was going well and what wasn't, where they needed help or maybe some input from the others. Finally we'd review our objectives and initiatives for the period and assess how we thought we were doing.' The exposing of personal information and gaining insight into each other's personality made the group closer and therefore facilitated more positive communication.

Good Witch or Big Bitch?

The Devil Really Does Wear Prada

Some corporations champion their bad behaviour. Long before the book *The Devil Wears Prada* came out, it was common knowledge that editors who worked at Condé Nast magazines called themselves 'Condé Nasties'. The sad truth was that, not only were human resources party to the misery, they even perpetuated it. Krista Dale was a young editorial assistant with almost four years' experience when a magazine sale found her interviewing for a job at Condé Nast. After failing the requisite typing test (on a typewriter, by the way), she was told by the human resources manager that she had 'no skills', and was offered a position as the second editorial assistant to the editor-in-chief of a fringe magazine for more than $10,000 *less* than the $28,000 she was making at her last position. When asked how people could survive on that kind of income, the human resources manager told her that her editorial assistants didn't work 'because they needed the money'. At least she was honest.

The lesson? Know the culture you're going into. Learning a new job is hard enough without added pressures.

Girl Talk: Gretchen Monahan

Gretchen ('Gretta') Monahan is building a small empire of salons, day spas, and fashion boutiques in the Boston area, and appears regularly as a make over coach on the US TV channel TLC's A Makeover Story. Gretchen took out a loan in 1995 to start Grettacole (www.grettacole.com), and today she has approximately 110 employees and six businesses, including two full-service salons and day spas, two Gretta Luxe fashion boutiques, and G Spa, which provides 'quickie' spa services. Gretchen also offers women personalized online consultations with tips on hair, make-up, skin treatment, and clothing.

In 2000, Gretchen was one of Boston's premier stylists and the self-styled 'star' and owner of her flagship salon,

Grettacole, in Wellesley, Massachusetts. She worked 80 hours a week 'doing heads' and training and managing a team of stylists. When she opened her second salon, she simply split her 80 hour a week into two 40s, one in each salon. As the salons became more and more successful, others soon followed. She began to believe that her dream of launching a national style brand could be attained, but things would have to change.

First, she would have to pull herself out of the salon, stop doing hair, and become a leader of the team – a spokesperson for the company and an executive with a grasp of the finance and a vision for the future – a pretty tall order. So Gretchen sought out the support she needed to achieve her goals. Based on the advice of a mentor, she applied for and won a scholarship to the prestigious entrepreneur's MBA program at the Harvard Business School. We talked to Gretchen about her corporate culture and management style.

How would you describe your corporate culture?
We have a very high-touch business, are full of aspiration, and are focused on client care. We don't push paperwork, nor are we overly reliant on systems, although as we continue to grow this will change, too. The challenge is that change in salon culture takes years to achieve. We've been successful so far because we've proven that, if a stylist follows our programme and stays true to our core values of all-over client care, happiness, and satisfaction, then she will be more successful than in other salons and make more money.

How is your business organized?
Each business unit has a salaried manager, who is
responsible for the success of that business and all of the
people who work in it. At Grettacole, we don't just do
hair. We offer an integrated beauty and fashion
experience, and, because it is unique, both the team
members and clients need to be educated. I try to run the
organization as a family, as most of the senior
management team has been with me since the beginning
and has helped me develop the values and systems that
have made us successful.

*How do you communicate your vision and culture
to your employees?*
In the beginning I led completely by example. I touched
everyone. I trained every new member of the team and
met all of the clients, making sure their needs were met
and that everyone on the team, from the receptionist up,
offered our clients 'the Grettacole experience'. I realized
that this 'star' system was not scaleable and that I had to
find a way to communicate the Grettacole values to 110
employees in six stores, as well as to the hundreds of
clients in a very different way.

I had to abort mission on the star system, and pretty
darn quick. I offered my core team the opportunity to
become leaders. I asked them to put aside their fears of
abandonment and climb up the corporate ladder with me,
because there's a lot of room at the top. But more
importantly, I had to convince them that there was value
in the organization without the star. They had to trust

the training that I had given them for years and seize the opportunity to grow. As more time passed without me in the salon, they realized that they could continue the standards that we developed together. As the president and spokesperson, I can monitor, support, teach, and demonstrate, but I can't hold anyone's hand any more.

How have things changed for you and the business?
I'm proud to say the business continues to grow and prosper. The most drastic change has been in how we communicate with each other. I had always worked face-to-face, chair-to-chair, if you will; so switching to a predominantly e-mail and phone call communication was a huge change. We're now dependent on the computer managing our calendars, and communication with long-term senior members of staff is almost strictly by e-mail. I was in Milan, viewing the collections for Grettaluxe, when I got an e-mail from my assistant telling me that one of the original members of my team, Julie Deane, was going to be away from work because her son was diagnosed with cancer. Wow, I thought, and I am getting this horrible news in the middle of the night on my Blackberry. I wrote right back letting them know how sorry I was and that I could be home tomorrow if she needed me to fill in. The hard facts are that there are no balances in life, only trade-offs. I wasn't there in person for my friend. I spoke to her on the phone, and she told me to stay and work; they were okay, and she would check in with me via e-mail. Fortunately, her son has made an incredible recovery. What I realized is that in actual fact, I hadn't been communicating with her in person for some time. At Grettacole, we never interrupt a stylist when they

are with a client, and so when I call the store Julie rarely has time to come to the phone. We always e-mailed about work issues, and now we began e-mailing about personal issues. Tragically, a few days later, my mother died unexpectedly in her sleep. And Julie was there for me, with e-mails and phone calls and support. I'm very lucky. I started the company. I want the company to grow. I signed up for the long hours and the sacrifices, but only because of the accomplishments and skill of the team around me, am I able to achieve my goals and dreams. I try to remember that always. What I realized during the hard times is that life is precious and people are what matter. Sure, I will continue to work hard and accomplish my goals, but I try to keep it real too. I've seen too many CEOs or people on television begin to believe their own hype. They create their own star system and forget that their most valuable assets are their employees. The reality is that it is so much easier to go and do hair. You get instant, gratifying feedback from the clients, you can make lots of money, and your only concern is yourself. But that's not building a business, a business that can provide for the well-being of many other people. The discipline I now demonstrate will pay off for everybody in the future.

Office Politics Are a Big Fat Drag: Coping with Closed Doors, Whispers, and Rumours

We know: we thought we left this behaviour behind in high school. We assumed we'd grown up and moved on from the backstabbing and gossip, but, as we all now know, those passed notes and ruined reputations were just a dress rehearsal for the big show.

In the United States, *Glamour* magazine joined with www.lawyers.com to conduct a poll that revealed that 75% of women say we're tougher on other females than we are on men in the workplace. Of all the social institutions we graduate into, the workplace can be the worst kind of incubator for mean-spirited, ugly, and jealous behaviour that culminates in the lowest form of politics.

It shouldn't be this way, and women managers can change the tone and culture in today's workplace. The era of the old boys' club is coming to an end. According to the Center for Women in Business, 28% of women now earn more than their husbands. And women today represent 50% of the graduating classes in law schools, medical schools, and MBA programmes.

In 2000, CNN executive Gail Evans wrote a ground-breaking, best-selling book, *Play Like a Man, Win Like a Woman: What Men Know About Success that Women Need to Learn*. In the book, Evans put forth her thesis: women are not in star positions, because they haven't yet learned how to play the game. She believed that the game of business is played on a field where males have been comfortable since they were very young. She wrote, 'It's a game where winning is the obvious (and only) objective and where aggression, self-promotion, a tough skin, and an effective display of power are the signs of a winner. Women, on the other hand, enter the game disadvantaged, having been taught to be cooperative rather than competitive, to enjoy the process rather than simply the result, and to seek approval rather than assume success.' In her book, Evans set out to level the playing field by providing instructions on how men play, so that women can beat them at their own game.

Three short years later, she wrote a second best-selling book, *She Wins, You Win: The Most Important Strategies for Making Women More Powerful*, where she advises women to trump the old boys' network by playing a girls' game. She realized that it's not about playing games like men. It's about winning as women, and doing it together. Her rule in this book: 'Every time a woman succeeds in business, every other woman's chance of succeeding in business increases. Every time a woman fails in business, every other woman's chance of failure increases.'

As Gail Evans' new stance demonstrates, in a very short time women's power and sheer numbers have changed the rules in the workplace, but, make no mistake, the game is still on. And you had better know the rules. Playing politics takes time and energy from accomplishing your goals; it undermines the efforts of both you and your team, but sometimes you just can't avoid it.

The World Outside Your Office Door

Personality clashes, inter-departmental competition, sucking up to the boss, gossiping, acting one way with your team and another way with your management – these are just a few examples of office politics. According to the career planning section of www.about.com, office politics is an increasing problem, evidenced by a study from Accountemps: '18% of an administrator's time – more than nine weeks out of every year – is spent resolving conflicts among employees' ('Surviving Office Politics', *Talent Scout*, April 16, 1998).

Managers and employees who are spending more time playing politics are spending less time on their jobs – impacting on productivity and eventually the bottom line. Politics aren't just a big-company phenomenon. We've interviewed a number of people working in retail and restaurants (not too mention all of the postings we've seen on career advice websites and job complaint blogs) who've complained that the staff members who were 'most friendly' with the bosses got the best shifts and schedules. 'Bosses' pets' were held to a different standard from the other employees, and this created problems. It's impossible not to like some people more than others, but, as a manager, your responsibility is to make sure that your team has the tools and the environment to accomplish their work.

Terry Bragg runs a company called Peacemakers Training in Salt Lake City and works with organizations to create a workplace where people want to work, and with managers who want their people to work together better. In an article for *Occupational Hazards* (Bragg, 2004) magazine, he offered 'Nine Strategies for Successfully Playing Office Politics'.

1. **Be nice to everyone.** Don't believe the 'nice guys finish last' stuff. In office politics, nice guys build supportive relationships with other people. Bulldozers and sharks make enemies, and enemies make your life miserable by resisting and sabotaging you. Be sincerely nice to everyone, not just the people you think can help you. People resent phoniness.

2. **Be a team player.** A team player is someone who helps the team to achieve its goals, and helps other people to achieve their goals. Be a star by making other people look good, rather than taking credit for other people's achievements.

3. **Don't moan and complain.** Develop a reputation for being a problem-solver. Anybody can complain about a problem, but really valuable employees are those that prevent or solve problems. Although the squeaky wheel may get oiled, co-workers resent the whiny employee.

4. **Be visible.** You can't win office politics by hiding. You must be involved, and others need to perceive you as a valuable contributor at work. Get involved in solving important and highly visible problems. In the age of downsizing, many employees have been shocked to learn that they lost their jobs because upper management didn't know what they were contributing to their organization. You not only have to do good work; others must give you credit for your good work and perceive you as a good worker.

5. **Help your boss to succeed.** This is part of being a team player. It is also a smart strategy, because your boss is a major player in your promotability and in how upper management perceives you and your work. If you have a positive relationship with your boss, your boss is more likely to support your career and help you to advance. Now some of

you are reeling in disgust, because you hate your boss. Well, get over it. You will have a more difficult time winning at office politics if you openly declare war on or antagonize your boss. Remember, she probably kept her job and power-base because she knows a few things about playing office politics. You don't have to suck up to your boss, but you must nurture your relationship with him or her. If you disagree with your boss, do it privately. Be very careful about embarrassing your boss in public or in front of their superiors or staff. You don't want him or her trying to get even with you.

6. **Be loyal.** Avoid backbiting and backstabbing. Colleagues will support you if they believe that you will be there to support them. To get loyalty, show loyalty.

7   **Be good at what you do.** Develop your expertise and competence. Turn up on time and work hard for your full shift. To survive in the workplace, you need to do good work. If others perceive you as slack or incompetent, they will not support you. They will also resent your getting promoted before them.

8. **Mind your manners.** Be polite and courteous. Avoid being sarcastic or putting other people down. Err on the side of being gracious.

9. **Make other people look good.** We already mentioned this concerning being a team player, but it bears repeating. People will support you when they believe that you make them look good. They will resent you if they believe you take credit for the work they do. Give credit to others. Sincerely compliment others. Help people look important and successful in front of the people who are important to them.

Good Witch or Big Bitch

It's not always fair: some bitches get to the top
Jane and Sarah are two of the most successful saleswomen
in Chicago. They work for one of the hottest companies
in the industry and regularly exceed their sales goals. They
are loved by customers and other departments alike.
Unfortunately, they are miserable, and with good reason.
They work for a big bitch boss – a boss who regularly
breaks every rule in this book.

- She routinely eavesdrops on their conversations and
  berates them about the content. God forbid they are
  on a personal call: she will walk out of her office and
  into theirs, standing in front of them tapping her foot
  until they hang up.
- She requires Jane and Sarah to copy her in on all
  e-mails with outside customers so that she knows
  exactly what they are saying. It's distrustful,
  disrespectful, and makes them very guarded in
  everything they say.
- She screams regularly and for no apparent reason.
- She takes credit for their accomplishments with senior
  management – often with them in a meeting bearing
  witness.
- She places blame when things go wrong and never
  accepts responsibility.
- She is absolutely out of control when it comes to
  budgeting and managing costs, and never considers
  the big picture. She will regularly fly off the handle if a
  budget line needs to be increased even if another line is
  reduced to cancel out the overage.

- She will override their opinion in front of customers, their assistants, outside consultants, messengers, and pretty well anyone in the universe other than her own management, of course.
- Two excellent (reliable, smart, and friendly) department assistants sit outside Jane and Sarah's supervisor's office. She doesn't like their phone manner; they are much too friendly. She e-mails Jane and Sarah to ask them to be less friendly on the phone: 'They don't need to be so sweet, it wastes time.'

Jane and Sarah's supervisor was recently promoted and given more responsibility. In addition to all of those things they listed above, their manager is a master of politics. She has an uncanny knack for survival and has put her own needs and goals above all else, and so far it's been working for her. Her management has chosen to look the other way, because the department continues to produce. We believe her bad boss behaviour will catch up with her. We just hope it's soon enough for Jane and Sarah.

Girl's Guide to Gossip

In this book, we've interviewed experts about each subject we cover. We've included real-life stories of our own and from others. Kim is the world's living expert on workplace gossip – she's excelled at it, been burned by it, used it to her advantage, and was almost fired for it on a few occasions early in her career. She was never a malicious gossip, but she has the gift. She remembers people, faces, and places, and has an uncanny ability to put the pieces of a story together even when nobody tells her anything. She can listen to and participate in a number of different conversations at the same time, and, as an operator in the days before voice-mail, she would routinely answer the phones of 30 different people, getting to know each of their stories: who their friends and lovers were, what they liked for lunch, when they went to hair or personal fitness appointments, who their shrink was, and so on. She was friendly and chatty and occasionally passed on inappropriate information. Now she's a repentant gossip, and here's her hard-learned Girl's Guide to Workplace Gossip:

- Keep it to yourself. It's not easy, but when you learn a new piece of information, don't share it with anyone.
- Satisfy the urge with celebrities. Our favourite way to blow off steam and share gossip is to talk about celebrities – let's face it, their stories are always more exciting than your co-workers' or boss's will ever be.
- Set some boundaries and stick to them. You don't need to share every detail of your personal life. If you don't know what we're talking about, revisit Chapter 4.
- Being told positive news doesn't give you *carte blanche* to blab. Remember, it is not your story to tell. If a member of your team or your boss tells you they are pregnant, it is not information for you to pass on.
- If someone tells you something, assume that they don't want you to tell someone else.
- Being trustworthy can be your biggest asset. If you are a trusted member of an organization, you will be given more responsibility, more information, and more power.
- Don't ever use names in public. (For this one we have to credit Caitlin's husband, Andrew.) You just never know who you're sitting next to in a restaurant, on an aeroplane, at your child's school football match.
- Information is currency, but you don't have to treat it that way.
- If you overhear some information, don't pass it on. Remember, it may not even be true.

- Avoid negative talk. Complaining doesn't make things better and it usually makes them worse.
- If you have an idea on how to improve something, share it. Creating positive buzz can be very beneficial to an organization.
- If you do plan to pass something along, whatever you do, do not write it down (no e-mail!), ever. Pick up the phone. We try not to subscribe to the 'CYB' (cover your back) manual, however, in this case, we must. When you write something down, there is no denying that you said it. Written words including e-mails can be passed on and can never be denied. Trust us: CYB by not committing gossip to paper.
- If your role in the company puts you in contact with confidential personnel or financial information, keep it to yourself, for so many reasons: you can hurt people and the company and you will be fired for breaking confidentiality.

Don't Date Colleagues

We find that women fall into two camps when it comes to workplace dating: those who do, and those who don't. Our marines from Chapter 2 were a good example. Courtney had a policy against dating marines; Angela dated a marine (not in her chain of command) and wound up marrying him. Caitlin was an office dater. As a matter of fact, she too married her boss from a previous job. However, if she were to do it all over again, she probably would try and avoid workplace dating. Not only did she have to find another job to continue her relationship, but when her team found out, she became an instant pariah. Being a pariah is bad, but being the subject of a lawsuit is certainly worse.

In a ruling that significantly expanded the law on sexual harassment in the American workplace in 2005, California's Supreme Court ruled that workers can sue when a colleague who is sleeping with the boss is shown repeated preferential treatment.

According to the *New York Times*, 'Unions and lawyers who represent workers rejoiced, claiming a victory for a group some of them call "the unloved". Phil Horowitz, chairman of the California Employment Lawyers Association, said employees can no longer be "treated as second-class citizens because they're not putting out".'

Lawmakers in other states are looking at this ruling and considering recommending similar legislation. Think twice before dating a colleague, and it's probably better to just avoid dating the boss, especially if he's married. You may think this is common sense, yet it happens all the time. It's also important to remember that society's acceptance of women dating in the workplace or cheating on their husbands is a lot lower. If a woman is going to try and date the boss, she had better be sure that it's going to be worth it. The American journalist Suzy Wetlaufer may have got Jack Welch – the former CEO of General Motors – to leave his wife and marry her, but she also lost her job and had to weather being trashed in the newspapers and on television for months. There is no comparable legislation in the United Kingdom at the time of writing, but it is an area to treat with extreme caution nevertheless.

Managing Your Manager

As an employee, when faced with a highly political environment, you can do a few things to make life easier for yourself and with your supervisor. A number of managers, when sharing their experiences, unwittingly shared their frustrations about their staff. Like communication, frustration is a two-way street. We've culled all of the frustrations, thrown in our own, and come up with a list of things to help you to be a better employee. If you honour your side of the bargain, we can guarantee you will be better managed.

- It's not about you. You are not the most important cog in the wheel and should not be the focus of everyone's attention. Consider your role and try to look at your manager's challenges in addition to your own.
- Get to know your boss's challenges and help to solve them. If you become known as a problem-solver, your boss will give you more responsibility and better assignments and quicker promotion.
- Make yourself useful. If you see something that needs to be done, do it. An 'it's-not-my-job' attitude gets you nowhere with your management.
- Know your boss's schedule and try to work within it. For example, if you know that she has a weekly meeting with her manager on a certain day, then communicate your accomplishments and challenges to her the day before.
- Be loyal. If your manager has treated you fairly and with support, you owe her some allegiance.
- A little initiative goes a long way. Every single manager we interviewed said they preferred employees who took chances and made mistakes to those who waited and regularly asked for instruction.
- Know the pecking order. If you're a new employee, the chances are you're at the bottom of it. Don't worry, we've all been there.
- If you're unhappy, speak up. Be specific about the problems you're having and try to come to the conversation with some solutions.

The High Road Less Travelled

It's pretty boring, and it's never easy, however the best advice we can offer you is this. To be successful in office politics, take the high road. If everyone around you is being negative, keep your mouth shut. If someone shares a juicy piece of gossip with you, don't pass it along. If the office hours are flexible, and most people show up late, get in on time. Maintain friendly relationships with everyone, even if you can't stand them.

Go ahead and blog: you may just get fired for it

We've established that you can be fired for dating your boss and coming in late. That seems pretty obvious compared to the newest craze in the category of fireable offences: blogging about your workplace. Only a few will able turn their blogs into six-figure book deals and movie options. So, most likely, what worked for Jessica Cutler, author of *The Washingtonienne* and famous blogger, who got fired from the post room in the office of Senator Mike DeWine after sharing her experiences of trading sex for money with high-profile Washington politicos, will not work for you. As she herself said when interviewed in the *Washington Post* when the scandal broke, 'I was only blogging for, what, less than two weeks? Some people with blogs are never going to get famous, and they've been doing it for, like, over a year. I feel bad for them.'

For those of you who are not blogging about being paid for sex by politicians but merely complaining that your boss and co-workers are lazy and irritating, take heed. You can and probably will be fired if someone from your workplace reads it. According to an article in *USA Today* in 2005, 'Delta Air Lines, Google, and other major companies are firing and disciplining employees for what they say about work on their blogs, which are personal sites that often contain a mix of frank commentary, freewheeling opinions, and journaling.'

Blogs are everywhere. According to a report this year by public relations firm Edelman and Intelliseek, a provider of business-intelligence solutions, about 20,000 new blogs are created daily. It was estimated that ten million U.S. blogs would have come into existence by the end of 2005. Together, these blogs link up to create what is known as a blogosphere, a collective Internet conversation that is one of the fastest-growing areas of new content on the Web.

Workplace blogging can be scary territory. Employees who create blogs set up a direct way to communicate about their company with the public, because customers and clients can stumble across a blog when doing a seemingly harmless Google search. And isn't that rather the point? You're not blogging for yourself – that could be done on the private hard-drive of your computer – you're blogging so other people will read it. And, if other people read about incompetence in your workplace, inter-office affairs, new projects that you're working on, you can put your employer and yourself at risk.

Because blogging is so new, laws specifically relating to it haven't been written yet, and companies are just beginning to write their policies. There are, though, existing laws of libel and defamation, so tread carefully. We recommend using common sense when blogging.

- Don't complain, libel, or otherwise disrespect people who you work with.
- Don't blog about your sex life, your drinking habits, or your recreational drug use. Some companies even have 'morals clauses', and if you break them – even in your own time – you will be fired.
- Don't assume you're anonymous. The more salacious your blog, the more people who read it will try to work out who you are.
- Don't blog about the projects you are working on – this could be considered privileged information by your employer.

Of course, if you can't blog about any of the above, there may be no reason to blog at all – which is the safest route.

Girl Talk: Franke James

Franke James describes herself as an artist/inventor/writer and a founder of www.office-politics.com. She has been developing new creative products, everything from games to cartoons, since 1997. She's designed light-hearted 'psychological' and satirical Internet games. The Office-Politics site was conceived in 2000 as a place where people could turn for information, advice, and entertainment about all things office-political. People love the free advice column, and she's received thousands of posts from all over the world and from all kinds of industries. To handle the volume, she's assembled a growing list of authors, executive coaches, and ethical experts. Her latest project is the Office-Politics® game. Franke shares her experiences of office politics with us.

What is the most common dilemma you hear?
Nobody appreciates all the work I do.

In the Office-Politics® game, many of the situations you present are much more serious than office politics. You cover harassment and petty white-collar crime and a number of basic ethical situations. What parameters should be put on office politics v. more serious offences?
Office politics is about the ethical culture and values that everyone in the office shares (or doesn't share!). So, you have to ask yourself, 'What are the important values in my office? Do I fit in? Is openness and honesty encouraged, or is lying, cheating, and bribery the unspoken rule?'

Depending on who you are and what your values are, you are going to be a fish out of water in one office or swimming happily in another. Obviously most offices are not that black and white; there is a huge scale, but it's the old slippery slope. Is lying okay when it's the executive secretary covering for the boss? Is lying okay when safety inspectors come to investigate a contamination problem because otherwise it will cause mayhem with the stock price? Is paying bribes okay because that's the way business is run in this country? It goes on and on.

I see office politics as encompassing all ethical, behavioural, and moral issues encountered in the office environment. It's about human nature. Family politics and school politics share many of the same dynamics.

Can you succeed in business without playing politics? If not, do you have any suggestions for how women can minimize the political landscape?
You can't escape office politics, but you can learn to play the game. Everyone has an agenda. Awareness makes all the difference. It's much better to understand how and why people are manipulating facts or events to bring about their desired outcome. Office politics are not necessarily evil. They are a fact of life and everyone is better off learning how to deal with them – and how to use them to their advantage!

People need to be asking themselves questions all the time, such as, 'How do my needs differ from the company's needs?', 'How are they in sync?', 'How can achieving my career objectives benefit the company?', 'Who in the company do I need to sell my idea to in order to make positive change happen?', 'Whose agenda will block my idea?', etc.

How bad does a situation have to get before you bring it to the attention of your supervisor or human resources?
Use your best judgment. Obviously, if it's a petty matter (e.g. who got the better chair, better holiday dates, etc.), then you should rise above it so you aren't branded as petty and small-minded.

But if it's a question of legality or harassment – sexual or psychological – don't wait. Life is too short, and the price of stress too high, to put up with a problem that's gnawing away at you or a co-worker.

What are your three absolute 'MUST NEVER DOs' in the workplace for women?

1. *Don't bitch about petty things.* Choose your battles so that you don't come off looking like squabbling children. Many bosses abdicate responsibility for deciding who is right and who is wrong. They are frequently impatient and just as likely to fire the innocent as the guilty.
2. *Don't do anything you wouldn't want to see splashed across the front page of the newspaper.* It's old advice, but good, especially in this age of mobile phones with cameras! Would Enron and Worldcom have had their respective meltdowns if their company culture had been zero tolerance for dishonesty?
3. *Don't mix office and romance.* This is a tough one for many people. After all, we see our colleagues for more hours in the week than our partners. If you do succumb to temptation, have a good exit plan.

Are there strategies to adopt as managers to stop the politics before they can start?

Managers should hire for attitude, not ability. You can train someone to learn a new skill, but it's awfully hard to change ingrained attitudes (hmmm, brainwashing might work, but it's iffy). Attitudes set the stage for the company culture. The manager's hires should reflect the ideal company culture. This helps to create one big happy family where people generally embrace the same values (honesty, truthfulness, diligence v. lying, cheating, etc). That is true whether it's a good culture or a bad culture you want to build.

The Word: Elizabeth Spiers, Editor-in-chief

As founding editor of Gawker.com, a weblog about 'the darker Manhattan-centric themes: class warfare as recreational sport; pathological status obsession; and the complete, total, and wholly unapologetic embrace of decadence', Elizabeth became a celeb herself.

She is currently the editor-in-chief of the website mediabistro.com, whose mission is to 'provide opportunities (both on- and off-line) for you to meet each other, share resources, become informed of job opportunities and interesting projects, improve your career skills, and showcase your work'. She's also been a contributing writer and editor at *New York* magazine and a freelance writer for a number of publications. Her CV even includes a stint as a buy-side financial analyst focusing on small capital technological equities and early stage venture capital. She's been at the forefront of new media, has worked in traditional media, and even did a stint on Wall Street. Elizabeth shares some thoughts on blogging and office politics with us.

- People risk losing their jobs for blogging about work for the same reason that people write about work generally: it takes up half of your waking life. It's hard not to write about work. People who do it in such a way that it might jeopardize their jobs are usually just telling themselves that it's not a big deal or their boss won't find it.

- Perhaps because I've generally been good with office politics, I don't think they're a problem to be solved. There are hierarchies in every aspect of life, and they're not going to go away; so you'd best learn how to navigate them. Different kinds of workplaces have different kinds of problems. The things that made my life difficult when I was an equity analyst are not the same things that make my life difficult in the media industry.

- Working for Gawker was essentially the same as freelance writing. You're working from home and no one's really telling you what to do. Working in traditional media at New York magazine (though, to be fair, I was also blogging for them) was like having a nine-to-five desk job, except that, being a magazine, it was less rigorously bureaucratic than, say, a consulting or finance job. It's a creative pursuit and much more easygoing. I actually liked the magazine environment better, because being around other people was more stimulating than sitting on my couch all day with a laptop. There were other people I could learn from. Now I'm in a job that's environmentally more like a dot com, but my particular job is more similar to the magazine job than the Gawker job. I'm in the office all day, managing other people, assigning and editing stories, etc.

- The friend/editor boundaries are loose in my experience. I get together socially with many of my editors, past and present, and several of my bloggers and freelance writers have also become personal friends. You just have to be rigorous about setting boundaries, and, if there's any sort of conflict, you have to make sure they understand that you're doing your best to be sympathetic (and are probably more inclined to be, given your personal relationship), but you have your own job requirements. In situations where the personal relationship pre-dates your professional relationship, the general rule of thumb should be don't hire your friends unless you're capable of firing them, should that become necessary.

Being the Boss Without Being Bossy: Business Lessons You Learned in Childhood

Believe it or not, most people learn all they need to know about being the boss by the time they are five. Unfortunately, those basic principles that are written in stone while under the watchful eyes of our mothers, fathers, and teachers are all but lost once we are thrust out into the real world. But these forgotten nuggets are great tips for making it as an adult in the wonderful world of work.

Remember too-tall Tina who threatened you every day during break? She might have got your lunch money, but she never earned your respect. Think back to the little boy who copied off your paper in class? Well, he might have got an A in English, but we heard he got busted last year for insider trading. And that little telltale who told on you for passing notes in class? Well, yes, he is a hugely successful judge, but everyone hates him!

Sharing Is Caring

You didn't meet your sales goals, win the account, or take the company public alone, did you? On a daily basis, the individuals in your team bring their unique talents to the table and work together to accomplish professional goals. Yes, you guide the staff by making the plan, answering the questions, and settling the disputes. But they are still working, contributing, and creating on behalf of the company – and you will not inspire them to do any of it well if you treat them as just a cog in your wheel. It takes a confident manager to step aside and give credit where credit is due. Nothing will inspire loyalty like a boss who acknowledges that she didn't do it flying solo.

Along with sharing credit, effective managers need also to share information. If you are busy, it is easier to deliver pieces of only the most time-sensitive information. But you are doing your team a disservice by not sharing the whole picture. When delegating a project, tell your team how it fits into the company's goals. If your CEO has decided to launch a new identity campaign or new product, then tell your staff about it. If there is a bad review coming out for the restaurant you manage, make sure to tell the staff. Information helps your team do a better job in both the short run (day-to-day tasks) and the long run (professional goal setting). It helps them to plan, grow, and think big picture.

She Did It!

If the team makes a serious mistake then the good boss takes the blame. That is the way it should be. Your power and salary are higher than those of everyone below you on the corporate ladder for a reason. It is really your future, and possibly your job, on the line when a project goes wrong. Eating humble pie can be frustrating when it was your assistant who forgot to send the presentation, but that goes with the territory. Imagine what your boss would think of you, if, when criticized for something, you pointed at your fresh faced assistant and said, '*She* did it!'. When helping her boss with an event, Ilene Kramer, an assistant to a high-profile event planner, mistakenly ordered 500 not 5,000 invitations. When she found out, her boss said it was a huge mistake but worked with her to fix it. When the client called, she let her scream, soaked it up, and apologized on behalf of the company. Because she had protected her employee and partnered with her to solve the problem, she earned her respect and, more importantly, her loyalty. It takes self-confidence to take the bullet for the team, but have faith that, by taking responsibility, your boss and direct subordinates will respect you for it.

The Word: Amy Costello, Kindergarten Teacher

Amy Costello is a kindergarten teacher and a mother of two. We spoke to her about what she tries to teach the kids in her care and were shocked by how applicable it all was to the workplace. We think Amy would make an amazing corporate mentor and manager.

- If Rachel did something that bothered Jimmy, then I encourage him not to talk to other people about it and not to dwell on it, but rather to bring it up directly with her. I find that children will immediately come to me or talk to their friends when something has hurt them, but they rarely talk to the instigator about it first.
- I teach kids to be organized. I work with them to create a place for everything such as homework, jacket, hats, and mittens. Everything we do at this stage is about setting up good habits.

- We want the children to learn to take responsibility for themselves, their work, and the impact they have on the world around them. The buck stops with them; so, if they lose their homework, it isn't okay to say, 'My mum forgot'.
- I think it is really important that all of the kids have a goal to work on. At the beginning of the school year, I sit down with each of them and set a goal. For one it could be learning to tie their shoes, for another it could be learning to read additional words. It helps to keep them focused on something, and the sense of achievement they have when the goal is achieved is a wonderful thing for their self-esteem.
- They have to learn to be on time. We don't want anyone to think it is okay to be late to their desks, groups, or classes and so we teach them to look at the clock.
- I try and teach them that a positive attitude is everything. We play a little game and for a day they go about their lives seeing if their smile will get a smile back. When they realize that almost everyone they encounter smiles back, they understand how much of an impact their attitude has on the people around them.
- We want all of them to understand that we are all different and that everyone has strengths. We encourage the children to work together to make the most of these strengths. If Jonathan is having a hard time with writing his 'A's, we set him up with Jennifer, who has great handwriting. If Jennifer is having a hard time organizing her locker, then we ask Ethan to give her a hand, because he is very neat.
- We teach them to take pride in their work by having them redo it if it is sloppy or if I know they can do better.
- The only mistake they can make with me is not trying.

Don't Be a Know-all

Yes, the chances are that you know the answer and the best way to do things. And, yes, your ideas are most likely smarter than the ones that your team comes up with. But so what? That is why they pay you the big bucks. To empower your people, you need to listen and make them feel heard. In brainstorms get their ideas, in meetings ask their opinions, and in reviews respect their point of view. If you have gathered a diverse, intelligent group of people to support you, then their contributions are only going to add to a proposal, presentation, or new product development. If you do solicit ideas, remember that occasionally you need to implement them. Donna Lynn, a nurse at a city hospital, told us that every month her supervisor asks everyone for their ideas on how to tweak management and improve schedules. After a few months of stuffing the ideas box with what the nurses thought were excellent suggestions and noticing that literally not one was implemented, they gave up. 'It quickly became obvious that they were just playing at management, trying out something they had read in some book. They didn't really care about us or our ideas.' Don't just pay lip service; your team will catch on quickly.

One Face is Better Than Two

So, your boss is an ineffectual, unlikeable bitch, and you would like nothing better than to share that with everyone you meet. Just because you would like to, doesn't mean that you should. If you don't like your boss, then work on changing how she treats you or move on. Those are your only options. Being negative by complaining about her to your staff sets a bad precedent. You are demonstrating to them that it is acceptable to be disrespectful, and complaints about you could be just round the corner. Backstabbing can cause you to lose your job, because, as is the case with most gossip, your complaints could get back to her. Just as important is not backstabbing your employees. Your options are similar: either try and improve the working relationship or fire them (see tips in Chapter 3). Talking behind someone's back occurs when one person doesn't want to confront the other. It is a weak and borderline dishonest manoeuvre that won't win the respect of the people around you.

Always Tell the Truth, Even When It Hurts

As a manager, you need to respect what that role represents to those above and those below. Your boss has entrusted you to be frank with them about what is going on with your team and your successes and failures. Don't lie to them about sales you haven't made, projects you haven't finished, employees you haven't yet reviewed. If you are less than honest, even once, they will begin to question all of the information you are presenting to them. This also holds true for the team. Be honest with them about how they are doing, share customer feedback, and let them know if the company is on target with goals. Obviously, you don't tell them proprietary information, but always tell them the truth. Even if the feedback is negative, there is a professional way to present it to your employees. Telling the truth is harder sometimes than not; so the manager who is striving to be a leader should always be honest.

Miss Manners: Say Please and Thank You

'There's no excuse for bad manners.' How many times have we heard that? It was good advice when first said and it is good advice now, although some managers may have forgotten. *Phoenix Business Journal* reported that in a study conducted by etiquette consultants Eticon Inc., 80% of the respondents reported an increase of rudeness in business. When they encounter rudeness, 58% of the people surveyed said they will take their business elsewhere. 'Rude behaviour ruins business,' said Ann Humphries, Eticon president.

A number of good books have been written on business etiquette that will help you brush up on your skills. We like *The Etiquette Advantage in Business: Personal Skills for Professional Success* by Peggy and Peter Post (third generation of Emily Post); *Power Etiquette: What*

You Don't Know Can Kill Your Career by Dana May Casperson, and *Manners That Sell: Adding the Polish That Builds Profits* by Lydia Ramsey.

Here are some tips from Lydia Ramsey on making a good first impression.

- Remember that you are always on stage. At any given moment you may encounter that sought-after client or potential employer. Always be prepared to look and sound your best.
- Focus on the other person. Use the person's name immediately in conversation.
- Smile and make eye contact. You will make other people feel good about themselves and about you.

Stealing Stinks: Keep Those Hands Out of the Cookie Jar

Of course we're not talking about removing people's property. That is obviously and horribly wrong. What we're talking about are the two common forms of theft in the workplace: stealing ideas and stealing time.

Ideas stealers don't last long. Eventually they will be caught. They may get away with it for a while, but those you are stealing from will catch on fast, and soon there will only be silence when you're in the room. Sooner or later, you've got to stand on your own and either do the job or not. Taking other people's ideas – like taking credit for their work – is not for anyone who wants to be a good manager. Working with people on good ideas is a different story.

Sitting at your desk checking personal e-mails, instant messaging friends, planning holidays, or shopping for bargains, if done regularly, is stealing time from your organization. And stealing time means stealing money. The long hours that many of us keep now require us to handle personal business while we are at our workplace. However, as managers, it is important to set an example. Don't abuse the privilege or allow your staff to either. Keep track of how much time everyone is losing to personal business, and, if it gets out of control and work begins to suffer, start banning personal time on the computer.

Just Say You're Sorry

As Hugh Grant proved when he apologized on The Tonight Show with Jay Leno for cheating on his then-girlfriend Elizabeth Hurley with a prostitute, no mistake is so big that an apology can't cure it. During her insider trading scandal, legal analysts were begging Martha Stewart to apologize. She refused, and went to jail.

Not all apologies are created equal, however. In *Psychology Today*, Dr Aaron Lazare suggests that there is a right and a wrong way to offer a sincere apology. If you don't include some crucial elements, your apology is likely to fail.

Here are the components of a good apology.

- Be specific and take responsibility for the impact of your transgression. 'I'm sorry for my mistake' is not enough. 'I am sorry that I sent an unapproved press release out to the media and jeopardized our client' is better. It acknowledges that you know what you did wrong and why it's important.
- Explain why you messed up, and let the injured party know that you learned from your mistake and that it won't happen again.
- Make sure you communicate that it wasn't personal, so that you can regain trust in the relationship.
- You have to show a little suffering: for your apology to be believed, the injured party has to be able to see you sweat a little. It shows them that this situation really matters.

Finally, nothing undermines a good apology more than repeatedly making the same mistake. We have a member of staff who is always late. Almost every day, she comes in with a heartfelt apology and excuse for her tardiness. We've lost interest in both the apologies and the excuses. We simply want her to get to work on time.

Good Witch or Big Bitch?

Why is she so crazy?

Jennifer Mitchell moved to New York from San Francisco to take a job at a marketing company, where, unbeknown to her, there'd been several rounds of redundancies in the year prior to her arrival. She realized pretty quickly that she'd landed in a bitter and deflated environment composed of paranoid employees. Here's her story.

On my first day, my boss, 'Linda' took me to lunch, and, by the time we finished our sandwiches, I knew of the dozens of shortcomings my colleagues allegedly possessed. It was a little unsettling, especially when she used words like *incompetent* and *clueless* about a vice president named 'Paul' she'd inherited when the technology department had dissolved. Even stranger, she instructed me to supervise Paul, despite his seniority to me.

After a few weeks as Linda's Golden Girl, the other shoe dropped. I expected it would, given the way she spoke about my colleagues, but never imagined how bad it would get. Looking back, it seemed to start when my team had to move to the other end of the office. Instead of moving me with them, she put me in an office that was a good 30 second (brisk) walk from Linda and the rest of the team. Linda was rarely in her office, which I'd soon discovered after making trips back and forth several times a day. I'd go days at a time without seeing her, and it began to impact on our relationship. She also frequently withheld critical information about our company and my clients, and didn't invite me to several important meetings, only then to accuse me of negligence and lack of commitment to my work. I explained that, as a result of her busy schedule, I hadn't had access to some important information and meetings, that I'd had no way of knowing about x, y, or z, and would like it if we could set up a weekly one-to-one and/or e-mail update to ensure that we were on the same page. 'I'm not your mother, Jennifer, and I can't be expected to hold your hand. You need to be more proactive,' was her response.

A few weeks after the move, she began to find fault with virtually everything I did. By the way, an important thing to note is that Paul, the incompetent, clueless VP, had been moved to an office next door to Linda's. Suddenly they seemed to be very chummy, and my initial paranoia about them conspiring to push me and a couple of other colleagues out was soon confirmed.

I took a late evening call on my mobile from clients in California who'd just received a final and long-awaited government approval and urgently wanted to meet me in person to ramp up. They thought that, since I was going to San Francisco (home) for Thanksgiving, it would be ideal to extend the trip by one day so that I could go to their offices for a meeting. Well trained by that point, and paranoid that they reached me directly without reference to Linda, I made no commitment other than saying I'd discuss it with Linda and the team and get back to them. I immediately left detailed voicemails for both Linda and Paul. At 10 pm that night, Linda called my apartment. Thankfully, my boyfriend was there for this conversation, because I'm not sure anyone would have ever believed it. In a nutshell, she not only accused me of breaking specific and 'official' orders about client contact, but she also said the following:

'I am stunned and appalled by your behaviour today.'

(When I asked her if she'd checked her e-mail and voicemail to fully understand the nature of the conversation I'd had, she said, 'That's irrelevant.')

'Jennifer, I'm no psychologist, but I would honestly suggest you seek some help to figure out what your motives are for your behaviour. You seem to be very troubled young woman.' After about ten minutes of other attempts to make me feel awful and reconsider whether the company was a good fit for me, she said: 'And, in addition, I have documented evidence that you broke into my e-mail account and read and deleted my e-mails on a few occasions.'

At the end of this call, she said the most important thing was for me to have a wonderful Thanksgiving with my family. And by the time I arrived in SF the following day, she'd left three messages on my mobile phone, the last one to this effect:

'Jennifer, I just wanted to say thanks again for your hard work and efforts with the client yesterday. Please don't worry about scheduling a meeting while you're in the Bay Area. It's your vacation, and I want you to enjoy it. But you did great work, thank you. And we'll see you when you get back to the office.'

Needless to say, I resigned upon my return, with as much grace as I could muster, keeping faith in karma whenever I fantasized about submitting a first person account with real names to a trade magazine. When Linda called a staff meeting to announce my resignation, she couched it as a very disappointing piece of news and said that I was a very talented specialist and would be missed.

Big Bitch. This boss was clearly paranoid, manipulative, unprofessional, and untrustworthy. She should not have been put in charge of anything, never mind anyone. She is the type of backstabbing, game-playing headcase that gives the rest of us women managers a bad name. We can't imagine that her career went far.

Don't Be a Bully: Being the Boss Doesn't Make You King (or Queen) of the Castle

According to the Workplace Bullying and Trauma Institute (yes, it really does exist; see www.bullyinginstitute.org), an abusive boss is more likely to be a woman than a man. Woman to woman bullying represents 50% of all workplace bullying; man to woman is 30%; man to man 12%; and woman to man bullying is extremely rare: only 8%.

Dr Harry Levinson, the dean of organizational psychologists and head of the Levinson Institute in Waltham, Massachusetts, admits that there has been no comprehensive study of bully bosses. However, organizational psychologists agree that they exist. After almost 40 years in consulting with companies, he has identified the common characteristics of bully bosses. 'Bully bosses over-control, micromanage, and display contempt for others, usually by repeated verbal abuse and sheer exploitation. They constantly put others down with snide remarks or harsh, repetitive, and unfair criticism. They don't just differ from you, they differ from you contemptuously; they question your adequacy and your commitment. They humiliate you in front of others.'

The Workplace Bullying and Trauma Institute has categorized the bullies. Take a look at them and make sure you don't fit the bill. If you do fit any of these bullying types, then you might want to consider taking an anger management course or speaking to human resources about signing you up for a leadership workshop. The bottom line is that you can't lead effectively if you bully your employees.

- *Constant critics* use put-downs, insults, and name-calling to intimidate. If this is you, then put yourself in your employee's place. Would this motivate you? We didn't think so.
- *Two-headed snakes* pretend to be nice, but all the while they're trying to sabotage the team. No one likes a backstabber. Your team is counting on you to be upfront with them, good, bad, and ugly.
- *Gatekeepers* are obsessed with control. They allocate time, money, and staffing to assure their target's failure. Control freaks ultimately want to control subordinates' ability to network in the company or to shine. If this is you, then you most likely have noticed your constant stream of assistants. If they succeed, you succeed.
- *Screaming Mimis* are emotionally out of control and explosive. You need help if this is you; so sign yourself up for an anger management class – ASAP.

Play Fair: Cheats Never Win and Winners Never Cheat

We live in a world of cheats. We cheat on our taxes. We cheat on our spouses. We cheat on our diets. David Callahan, author of *The Cheating Culture: Why More Americans Are Doing Wrong to Get Ahead*, the first exhaustive look at the cheating in America, explains on his website, www.cheatingculture.com, that more people cheat now because the pressure to succeed is so much higher, starting at an earlier age. Any parent in New York City will tell you that, if you don't get your children into the right pre-school, they will never get into the right college. He also concludes that, if you cheat and get away with it at a young age, you're more likely to cheat as an adult and in your workplace.

Companies and managers need to adopt zero-tolerance policies for cheating. In the post-Enron, -WorldCom, and -Tyco world, organizations need to be vigilant about telling the truth and representing their finances accurately to their employees and the public. Fudging budgets, padding expense reports, and fixing time cards are disciplinary offences that will lead to termination.

Girl Talk: Linda Greenlaw

Linda Greenlaw loves fishing. She is the only woman ever to captain a swordfishing boat, working the waters east of the Grand Banks of Newfoundland. She captained the *Hannah Boden*, the sister boat of the *Andrea Gail*, that was made famous in the book and film *The Perfect Storm* by Sebastian Junger. Junger described Linda as 'one of the best captains, period, on the entire East Coast'. Starting out as a cook and deckhand aboard a swordfishing boat during her summer breaks from Colby College in Maine, Linda had worked her way into the captain's chair by 1986.

She traded in her captain's chair on this boat for her own lobsterboat. She works it with her father inshore, fishing the water surrounding her home on Isle Au Haut, a small island off the coast of Maine. She has written four books, all published by Hyperion (see Extra Help: Resources), including, most recently, *Recipes from a Very Small Island*, which she has written with her mother.

With the exception of her book publicist and her mother, she has never worked for, with, or around women. There were no women crews, and no woman has ever asked her for a job. Linda's professional experience is unique, yet she described lessons that will benefit us all.

Why were there no women in your professional life?
Commercial fishing is not an industry on the rise. More people are getting out, not getting in, and I think it is a job that young women today wouldn't even consider. All

the people involved with the fishing industry – the ones who buy fish, sell fish, sell bait, and handle the gear – are men. Fishing is my first love. I didn't care that I was surrounded by men, because all I cared about was my own performance.

Can you describe your management philosophy?
And how did you develop it?
I never thought about a philosophy per se, but I suppose if I had to come up with one, I would say that I treat people the way I want to be treated. I don't enjoy people who are bossy or loud and so I don't act that way.

I started at the bottom – you can't get much lower than a cook on a fishing boat. I was the 'green guy' (lowest hand) on the boat when I was 19. I worked for some men who were screamers, and I've worked for and around men who are gentlemen. It's been a 50-50 proposition. I would imagine the boat is like everywhere else: some people are a lot easier to get along with than others, but, if you do the best that you can and treat everyone with respect, you'll have a better chance of succeeding.

We would imagine it was pretty difficult to be taken
seriously as a woman fisherman. How did you earn the
respect of the others?
I found something I loved to do. I worked very hard at it. I got good at it. Through the years, I worked at every job on the boat. When you ask most people their description of a fisherman, they describe a great big strong man. Most people think fishing requires brute strength. I've found that it is not about brute strength, but about

mental strength and physical endurance. As a 125-pound woman who stands at 5 feet 3 inches, I had to find new ways to do things.

I had a captain, Alden Leeman, nicknamed Screamin' Leeman, from whom I learned a lot about fishing and nothing at all about handling people. I worked for Alden first as a cook, then as a deck hand, and then as first mate. Becoming a captain in many ways is about staying on a boat long enough to get a chance. When Alden bought a second boat, he needed a captain and gave me the chance.

What qualities did you look for in your crew?
Looking for a job on a fishing boat is called looking for a 'site'. Guys would come up looking for a site, and I would ask questions: 'Can you cook?', 'Do you know this type of engine or refrigeration system?'

If there is one thing I know, it is that people lie to get jobs. I've found that the guy who says the least about himself usually turns out to be the best. The ones who are really trying to convince you how skilled they are never turn out to be the best workers. The guy who said, 'I'm a hard worker' was always the one I wanted on my boat.

Also, I didn't want input; I wanted work. I didn't care how they did it on another captain's boat. If they liked that way so much, they could go and work for them.

The best man to have on the boat was one who was capable of doing my job but who didn't want it. He wanted to be the best crew member he could.

And how did you find them?

If you're top producer, everybody wants to crew for you. If you're fortunate enough to surround yourself with the best people possible, you will be that much more successful. When I was running the *Hannah* boat, the Cadillac of the fleet, everyone just walked on and jumped into their role. A swordfish trip lasts 30 days; it is run by a five- or six-man crew and everybody works together. There's a butcher, someone to handle the tackle, an engineer, the first mate and the green guy or the cook. Everybody has to pay attention and there can't be one weak link. When there was a new person, he was never in charge of mission critical jobs. For example, he would never be in charge of cleaning fish. If the fish rot during the trip, it's a disaster. Green guys were charged with things that they could take a lot of pride in and were critical to the success of the trip, but couldn't lose us a lot of money or get anyone killed.

How did people react to a woman captain?

In the beginning it was funny. Some guy would come along the deck and ask me if my husband was aboard. When I told them I didn't have a husband, they would ask if the captain was aboard. When I replied that I was the captain, you could see the 'look' register on their face. They were thinking, 'Oh God, I guess I've blown it.' Once I got more established, it was never an issue.

It doesn't sound as if you needed to be a bitch to be respected. How did you do it?

I pride myself on not being a bitch. It takes a lot of work to be bitchy. If you're fishing it's a 24-hour exhausting job. Being a bitch would make it that much harder. I think I was successful because I worked harder. It's my nature to work hard, and gender never entered the picture. I never felt responsible for representing women. I represent only Linda Greenlaw. I just am myself and I don't want to be a role model. I love fishing and want to be good at it. Being a woman is something completely out of my control. It's simply a fact. Being a great fisherman is what I worked hard to do. Now I am putting my energy into doing the best job that I can writing and promoting my books. This may sound silly, but now I am fishing for readers and booksellers. I know if I do a good job for them, then they will do a good job for me and continue to support me and buy and sell more of my books.

A Final Note

We were recently invited to a fundraising gala for The Center for the Advancement of Women in New York, where we had the privilege of hearing both Gloria Steinem and Madeleine Albright talk about the importance of helping other women to succeed. Madeleine Albright said something along the lines of there being a special place in hell for women who don't help out other women, which got a big laugh, while at the same time inspiring all of us to think about the responsibility we have to our sisters.

We know this sounds a little 'I am Woman, hear me roar', but we really want to encourage all of you reading this book to be more mentor than manager, to be aware of your own internalized sexism, and to commit to not judging your female employees for not being more like the men in the office. Appreciate the diversity. Encourage your female employees to contribute and speak up, and support their professional growth and development along with that of your male subordinates. You have the opportunity to be the agent of change in your employee's life, to be their Good Witch story, and we hope that you make the commitment to master this challenging and sometimes wonderful role of being someone's boss.

Extra Help: Resources

Books we mentioned:

Leadership/Management

Autry, James A. *The Servant Leader: How to Build a Creative Team, Develop Great Morale, and Improve Bottom-line Performance.* Three Rivers Press, 2001.

Belbin, Meredith. *Management Teams: Why They Succeed or Fail.* Butterworth-Heinemann, 2003.

Blanchard, Ken, and Spencer Johnson. *One Minute Manager.* Collins, 1983.

Blanchard, Ken, and Patricia Zigarmi. *Leadership and the One Minute Manager.* Collins, 1999.

Glaser, Judith. *Creating We: Change I-Thinking to WE-Thinking & Build a Healthy, Thriving Organization.* Platinum Press, 2005.

McBee, Shar. *To Lead Is to Serve.* SMB Publishing, 2002.

Templar, Richard. *Rules of Management.* Prentice Hall, 2005.

Women/Business

Evans, Gail. *Play Like a Man, Win Like a Woman: What Men Know About Success that Women Need to Learn.* Broadway Books, 2000.

Evans, Gail. *She Wins, You Win: The Most Important Strategies for Making Women More Powerful.* Gotham, 2004.

Weisberger, Lauren. *The Devil Wears Prada.* Doubleday, 2003.

Inspirational Memoirs

Greenlaw, Linda. *The Hungry Ocean: A Swordboat Captain's Journey.* Hyperion, 1999.

Greenlaw, Linda. *The Lobster Chronicles: Life on a Very Small Island.* Hyperion, 2003.

Greenlaw, Linda. *All Fisherman Are Liars.* Hyperion, 2004.

Greenlaw, Linda. *Recipes from a Very Small Island.* Hyperion, 2005.

Junger, Sebastian. *The Perfect Storm: A True Story of Men Against the Sea.* W. W. Norton, 2000.

Etiquette

Casperson, Dana May. *Power Etiquette. What You Don't Know Can Kill Your Career.* American Management Association, 1999.

Post, Peter and Peggy Post. *The Etiquette Advantage in Business: Personal Skills for Professional Success.* Collins, 1999.

Ramsey, Lydia. *Manners That Sell: Adding the Polish That Builds Profits.* Longfellow Press, 2000.

Entrepreneurship

Friedman, Caitlin and Kim Yorio. *The Girl's Guide to Starting Your Own Business.* HarperCollins, 2004.

A few websites we mentioned in the book and more:

General Research
www.about.com
www.ivillage.co.uk

Etiquette
www.cheatingculture.com
www.cisleads.com

Blogs
www.iworkwithfools.com
www.fthisjob.com
www.oddtodd.com
www.revengelady.com

Women Leaders
www.guide2womenleaders.com
www.leadingfromthefront.com

Hiring and Firing
www.businesslink.gov.uk
www.dti.gov.uk
www.monster.co.uk

Entrepreneurship
www.onlinewbc.gov

Useful articles we mentioned in the book:

Bragg, Terry. 'Nine Strategies for Successfully Playing Office Politics', *Occupational Hazards*, 2004.
'Surviving Office Politics', *Talent Scout*, 16 April, 1998.

Index